Everybody's free to do what they want. We like the idea of having maybe one sound, but not having one style precisely. We record and do music the same way we used to, but we'd like to have an open mind. We like the idea Electronic and House music as being about destroying the old rules, and to set up new rules at the same time. We want to destroy the new rules as well. The labels and the categories were something that was set up by the system and by the media and the record labels to sell the music. 'Okay, so what are you? Are you Heavy Metal? Are you Soul? Are you Disco?' House was pretty much about destroying those barriers, but then now that it's accepted in a way, it's like are you Heavy Metal, or are you House music? If you're House music, then you have to do ten-minute soundtracks with one idea or two. It's interesting, but House music to us is more about the spirit that should be breaking those categories.

Thomas Bangalter

Behind The Music Tales Books

N.W.A: The Aftermath

The Real Eminem: Broke City Trash Rapper

The Real Destiny's Child: The Writing's On The Wall

New York State of Mind 1.0

The Reasonings of Buju Banton, Bounty Killer & Sizzla

Magnolia: Home of tha Soldiers (Behind the Scenes with the Cash Money Millionaires)

The Real 213

The Real MC Eiht: Geah!

The Real Diddy

The Real Daft Punk

The Artists Speak

"This guy! I plead the fifth. This guy is nuts."
- Eminem

"Dope questions, man. Very insightful, very thoughtful."
- G.U.R.U

"You like a Psychiatrist or some shit? This shit is just coming out but go ahead."
- Mary J. Blige

"Definitely a real interview! Digging deep up in there, man. Not afraid to ask questions!"
- K-CI Hailey

"The Wizard asked me for a copy of your magazine."
- Guy-Manuel de Homem-Christo

"You didn't wear your glasses, and you haven't carried your hearing aid. What else is wrong with you?"
- Bushwick Bill

"Peace and blessing, Brother Harris. Thank you for inspiring my words. Keep 'yo balance."
- Erykah Badu

"Can I see that pen?"
- Bobby Brown

"What else do you want to know? Talk to me."
- Aaliyah

THE REAL DAFT PUNK

HARRIS ROSEN

Behind The Music Tales

© 2018 by Peace! Carving and Harris Rosen.

All rights reserved. Aside from brief quotations for media coverage and reviews, no part of this book may be reproduced or distributed in any form without the author's permission.   hank you for supporting authors and a diverse, creative culture by purchasing this book and complying with copyright laws.

Published by Peace! Carving Mr. Heller Press

Heller HQ
QB
Spadina-Fort York
Toronto, ON M5V 2B3

behindthemusictales.com
facebook.com/behindthemusictales

First Edition: July 2018

ISBN: 978-1-988956-10-7 **(full-colour hardcover)**
ISBN: 978-1-988956-11-4 (paperback)
ISBN: 978-1-988956-03-9 (digital)

DEDICATION

TO MY SON AND MOTHER, FOR ALL THEIR LOVE

ACKNOWLEDGMENTS

Thank you, those who inspired me behind the scenes to produce this book. I appreciate your support, friendship, guidance, and understanding.

Twenty years ago, Gavin Gerbz was co-owner of Canada's legendary Industry nightclub. Together we blazed up the backrooms of clubs, restaurants and private residences with the leading lights of the electronic music revolution. His recollections, tales, and insight were instrumental to the initial version of this book.

My heartfelt thanks go out to James Watt for over thirty years of friendship and providing the keys for producing this book.

I am grateful to Craig "Stanley" Boyko for fifteen years of friendship, and always being there to assist or contribute to my projects and life.

I am grateful to Dennis Garces for twenty-five years of friendship, WMC 1997, and vital instruction on current affairs.

I am grateful to "Hey there, Rusty!" Russell Hergert for twenty years of friendship, and the official Virgin Records connection to Daft Punk in Miami and New York City.

I am thankful to "The Sizz" James Sharpe for offering to create a trailer for this book and delivering a sensational one.

I am thankful to Terence "Tee-Loo" Leung for taking time out of his busy schedule to design the first version of this book.

Salute to Mongoloids Junior Sanchez for his early assistance with this book, DJ Sneak for not mincing words and sparking the rewrite, and Armand Van Helden for taking time out of his schedule for multiple interviews and hangs in his Times Square home studio back in the day.

Salute to Kram, The Vintage Egg We Trust, CEO, Phil DeMetro, Moosh and the youths, Mr. Wilson, RGP, The K, Dr. David Esho, William J. Genereux, Eon Sinclair, Jr., Dennis Passley and the YellowCardPL Football chat crew. Shout out to the Unabomber Mario J on his lifelong journey to become the world's most fascinating man.

Respect goes out to Daft Punk Reddit community, Daft Punk Wikia, The Daft Club, Daft Punk Anthology, and Daft World for their vibrant spirit and valuable resources that were instrumental to the research and writing of this book.

Last but not least, thank you to the wonderful world of Adobe Creative Cloud. I hope to discover, learn and apply more of its offering to new books in the Behind The Music Tales series and beyond.

CONTENTS

PREFACE 12

INTRODUCTION 16

PART ONE: The Shit 39

THE REAL DJ SNEAK 47

BOOMER BROTHERS PRESENT DJ SNEAK'S BIRTHDAY BEATS 52

THE HISTORY OF DA MONGOLOIDS 60

PART TWO: Discovery 74

DISCOGRAPHY 98

WHO IS HARRIS ROSEN? 109

PREFACE

The Real Daft Punk embodies the dynamic practices and principles that launched Daft Punk to superstardom presenting the essence and gift of Thomas Bangalter and Guy-Manuel de Homem-Christo. A profound reflection of the tidal ebbs and flows of Dance Music intersected with divergent thinking. this book is honest behind the music tales of an exceptional brotherhood and the catalytic sea change fashioned by its comeuppance. Over two exclusive interviews with Daft Punk captured in the age of *Homework* and the gestation period leading up to and including the release of *Discovery*, *The Real Daft Punk* provides vital insight into how the duo achieved unparalleled success without compromising artistic integrity or musical vision.

With one love and one heart, the book chronicles the rise of House and Techno. In the words of its co-conspirators, drawing from my talks with Kevin Saunderson, Arthur Baker, Byron Stingily, Moby, 808 State, Underworld, and contributor interviews with Giorgio Moroder, Stacey Pullen and Cajmere/Green Velvet in the same time frame as the rise of Daft Punk. Adding the revealing tales of DJ Sneak and the notorious Da Mongoloids crew, who drew from the same wellspring of inspiration and included Daft Punk.

House Music rebels Armand Van Helden, Junior Sanchez, Roger Sanchez, Ian Pooley, Erick Morillo, Basement Jaxx, Bear Who?, Harry "Choo Choo" Romero, Unabomber Mario J, Rhythm Masters, Jacques Lu Cont. And others, who were early believers in enabling the maturation of the Art Form. DJ Sneak an early believer and significant supporter of Daft Punk after Thomas Bangalter handed him a promotional copy of *Trax On Da Rocks* in Paris. The sound of his filtered loops and disco mastery influential in the early output of Daft Punk.

Further setting *The Real Daft Punk* apart is over eighty original behind the music photos unmasking Daft Punk and their peers. Images from 1997, 2000, and 2001 Miami *Winter Music Conference*, the January 2001 photo shoot with Daft Punk in NYC, and others from inside clubs and interviews of the critical period in history.

The Real Daft Punk answering the questions who is Daft Punk? What is their purpose? Where did their unique sound originate? When did they begin to devise different music? Why do they prefer to remain anonymous? And how do they create tracks?

Many of you are wondering who is this guy from Canada independently publishing a book on Daft Punk? What qualifies him? Where and when did he get his source material? Why should I buy this book, and how did the book come together?

My name is Harris Rosen. I grew up with a voracious appetite for music, listening to community radio specialty shows, and buying vinyl weekly at new, used and import stores. I went to local shows weekly, driving and taking the train out of the city for festivals. Writing for the school newspaper, and helping to launch independent publications, I interviewed a wide range of artists. The likes of Jazzy Jeff & The Fresh Prince, Gene Simmons, Andrew Eldritch, Blur, Glenn Danzig, Henry Rollins, Motley Crue, Red Hot Chili Peppers, Sonic Youth, Metallica, Slayer, Gregg Allman, Malcolm McLaren, Jesus and the Mary Chain, and Nirvana, to list a few.

House Music played a prominent role in Toronto with devoted cubs and underground parties every weekend. New Jacks were graduating to Promoters bringing fresh vibes and rising genera to the city. Toronto's vibrant Rave scene primarily built by Scottish and British ex-pats selling mixtapes and throwing underground parties in 1990. Fast forward to spring 1992, and I published an interview with Chicago House artist Lidell Townsell. Attending Raves with an assortment of local DJ and out of town guests like New Atlantic, Speedy J, F.U.S.E. (Richie Hawtin), John Acquaviva, Mr. C, Rufige Cru (Goldie), and DJ Phantasy, and interviewing the likes of Ten City and Kevin Saunderson.

I started this book two years ago with new transcriptions and a few photo scans. It sat for over a year as I focused on creating and releasing past *Behind the Music Tales* titles. I've done it often, creating nine books utilising the archives I amassed as Publisher of *Peace! Magazine*. Digging into hundreds of hours of tape and thousands of photos documenting the rise of Hip-Hop and Dance Music throughout the 90s and 2000s. The collection is existing as a candid passage of knowledge recording the movement and thoughts of critical players within the Art Forms.

Motivated by a rediscovery of House and Techno music, I knew the seer words of its architects must assimilate into the world we inhabit. With Daft Punk, it was this and more. It has led me in the most unexpected and fantastic direction as I developed a new format to enter the behind the music tales of these significant artists who furthered Dance Music.

The book you are holding in your hands is the second version of *The Real Daft Punk*. The first was written and designed in the fall of 2017, with one hardcover copy printed to proof. Its designer, Terence Leung, a party veteran who crafted hundreds of flyers in the early days of Rave through the club era, said it was incomplete. He required more time to design, and indeed artists aside from Daft Punk included. He is right, and I thank him.

Initially, I put together a Keynote with four questions, sent it to Junior Sanchez and asked him to forward it to Da Mongoloids, which he agreed to do, and I am grateful. Nevertheless, I received no response, including Junior. Terence reconnected me with DJ Sneak, we spoke, and he committed. However, he soon dropped out too.

It's been twenty-one years since I interviewed Daft Punk for the first time. As I began to rewrite the book in its entirety, eventually more than doubling up its word and photo count, it came to me that I also had interviews with Da Mongoloids and many other crucial artists leading up to the era of *Homework* all the way through to the release of *Discovery*. The alternative of asking artists to recall the state of mind and music of an age replaced by real interviews from the period in question.

The source material of this book originating from my interviews with Kevin Saunderson (1992), Moby and 808 State (1993), Underworld (1996), Arthur Baker and Byron Stingily (1997), and contributor talks with Giorgio Moroder, Stacey Pullen, and Cajmere/Green Velvet (1998). The tale of Da Mongoloids captured in my 1996, 1997, 1998, and 2000 accounts with Armand Van Helden, Roger Sanchez (1997), and a contributor's 1998 interview with Ian Pooley. The DJ Sneak feature from our 1997 meeting.

The Real Daft Punk is much more than the narrative of Thomas Bangalter and Guy-Manuel de Homem-Christo exploding across international markets and opening up the Art Form to legions of new listeners. It is a story that, like its subjects, dismantles archaic unwritten rules of music industry conduct while providing the ideation necessary to lead a successful career as a confident creative with a rich legacy.

Introduction

The origin of Daft Punk dates back to 1992, and four songs of Beach Boys-inspired indie rock meets punk fabricated by Thomas Bangalter, Guy-Manuel de Homem-Christo and Laurent Brancowitz as Darlin'. "Cindy, So Loud" and "Darlin'" appearing in April 1993 on the white vinyl B-side of the eight-track UK double 7" compilation *Shimmies in Super 8* on the Duophonic label. Named after the audio signal processing of mono recordings to stereo by Capitol Records. Approximately 400 of its 800 copies carrying a Darlin' sticker and paper insert designed by Guy-Manuel de Homem-Christo. British weekly music newspaper, *Melody Maker*, tagged the music "a daft punky thrash," and the group disbanding the same year due to musical differences. The other two recordings "Untitled 18" and "Untitled 33" released in 1995 by Banana Split on the *De La Viande Pour Le Disco?* cassette.

Laurent Brancowitz picked up his guitar and joined his older brother, guitarist Christian Mazola, in synth-pop darlings Phoenix. Thomas Bangalter and Guy-Manuel de Homem-Christo bought drum machines and synthesisers and went to work as Daft Punk learning how to utilise them best.

The "Godfather of Techno" Juan Atkins and Eddie "Flashin'" Fowlkes @ WMC 1997.

Dance Music had always been around in various forms. "The Father of Disco," Giorgio Moroder playing with the Moog synthesiser as far back as the late 60s. His song "Son of My Father," recorded by Chicory Tip on Christmas eve 1971, in the studio of "Fifth Beatle" George Martin, is the first UK number one song to feature a synthesiser clearly. Moroder's taboo-breaking "I Feel Love," co-produced by Pete Bellotte for Donna Summer in 1977, widely recognised as one of the most influential songs of all-time originating electronic dance music (EDM) and the home studio revolution. Certainly one of the primary songs triggering the idea of people recording electronic music.

"I Feel Love" broke a lot of taboos," said Moroder in a 1997 interview with documentarian Iara Lee, director of feature-length *Modulations: Cinema for the Ear*. The film capturing a moment in history where humans and machines fused to create exciting sounds, and the history of electronic music.

"One is that people started to like that kind of music and then doing it, not in big studios, but starting to do it at home in small recording studios because it didn't need to have great musicians to write it. In fact, some of the major hits were done by numbers. So instead of people actually playing the song, they would dial in numbers. This whole electronic field of recording got a lot of incentives for people to record even in little demo studios because it opened a lot of people's new ideas. They didn't need all the money to record in a big expensive studio. That was one of the main reasons for the synthesiser to grow that rapidly."

The innovative sounds of Germany's Kraftwerk credited with popularising electronic instrumentation in the mid-70's, using synthesisers, vocoders, drum machines and self-made instruments. The surprise international chart success of the *Autobahn* album in 1974, laying the groundwork for electro-funk, ambient, and synth pop. Kraftwerk was branded "robot-pop" for the combination of pop melodies, sparse, repetitive rhythmic arrangements, and matching suits.

The 32-track Korg MS-10, known for its large electro bass, is arriving in 1978, the Roland TR-808 Rhythm Composer drum machine coming in 1980, permitting artists to create rhythms. Futurists Richard Davis and Juan Atkins forming Cybotron, the base of Detroit Techno, the same year. Drawing inspiration from Kraftwerk, George Clinton, Yellow Magic Orchestra, electro-pop, Italo-Disco, and the writings of Alvin Toffler focusing on the effects of modern technologies on global cultures. Atkins was also collaborating with teenage High-School friends Derrick May and Kevin Saunderson as Deep Space Soundworks. The trio became known as the Belleville Three, credited with developing the blueprint of Detroit Techno.

Juan Atkins, "The Godfather of Techno," going on to record Electro and Techno as Model 500 and Infiniti, starting the Metroplex label in 1985. Derrick May was releasing "Strings of Life," as Rhythim Is Rhythim on his Transmat label, in 1987. A song with no baseline that served to explode House and Techno in Europe. Acid House and Techno fueling what became the Rave scene. Symbiotically, the music spreading its wings leading to an infusion of new subgenera and sounds. Kevin Saunderson and Chicago vocalist, Paris Gray, topping the US Billboard Dance Chart twice in 1988 as Inner City with "Big Fun," and "Good Life." Twice in 1989 with "Ain't Nobody Better," and "Do You Love What You Feel," and once in 1992 with "Pennies From Heaven."

Chicago x Detroit.
Gene Farris and Kevin Saunderson @ WMC 2000

The revolutionary "Planet Rock" by Arthur Baker, John Robie, Afrika Bambaataa and the Soulsonic Force coming in April 1982. The melody is an interpolation of Kraftwerk's "Trans Europe Express," Yellow Magic Orchestra's "Rap Phenomena," Kraftwerk's "Numbers," and Ennio Morricone's *For a Few Dollars More* soundtrack. Along with its follow-up "Looking For The Perfect Beat" arguably the most influential songs, ever, credited as key to the development of Electro, Hip-Hop, Breakbeat, and the subgenera that followed. Baker and Robie as Planet Patrol creating "Play At Your Own Risk" on the remnants of "Planet Rock" the same year. Baker was moving on to co-produce "Confusion" with New Order in 1983, and "I.O.U." featuring Nikeeta in 1992, his other big hit.

"Everything comes around," said Arthur Baker in our spring 1997 interview. "What comes around goes around. What goes around comes around. Electro and that sound have come around three or four times since '82. Every few years someone discovers it again, and now it's sort of called Electronic. There's all this thing about the Chemical Brothers and all that kind of thing, but it's all - It's old electro Hip-Hop. It hasn't changed all that much. Maybe new drum sounds or something, but the basis is what we did in '82 and '81. When I'm in Miami, and I turn on Power(96), it's every three songs it's either a sample of one of my old records or one of my old records. It's cool. I'm glad the music's lasted. It stuck around probably because it was modern when we did it, and it hasn't dated all that much."

The programmable Korg Ploysix analogue synthesiser capable of producing multiple tones at the same time coming in 1982, and the 61-key, six voice polyphonic Roland Juno-60 later the same year. Its hybrid digital/analogue electronic oscillator used in synthesisers, micro-controllers, and software-defined radios. The standardised protocol for electronic instruments and computers to connect and communicate, MIDI, Musical Instrument Digital Interface, in 1983.

"If it wasn't for the technology, then nobody could be doing this style of music," said Kevin Saunderson in our summer 1992 interview, to promote his upcoming Inner City album, *Praise*.

Arthur Baker and Nadine Renee @ WMC 1997.

"I was one of the first people to be at the forefront of technology. The 808, the 909, the synthesisers. Even people like New Order, and Kraftwerk, and Depeche Mode, Pet Shop Boys. All those kinds of groups were dealing with electronic equipment as a different style. Our style was more for the dance audience and raw, and it was different because it was from Detroit and we had our vision. We brought it out. We made it known. But Techno was created by technology, because if you take it away what can you do really? You can't do it, can you? You have to play live and acoustic and sound like everybody else."

Acclaimed second-generation Detroit Techno artist, Stacey Pullen, who learned the ropes from Derrick May, spoke on the impact of Kraftwerk on the sound of Detroit and its Black community, in a 1997 interview with documentarian Iara Lee for her feature-length *Modulations: Cinema for the Ear*.

Stacey Pullen mesmerised on the WMC 1997 boat cruise.

"It was party music. It was real funky electronic party music, and the people in Detroit wanted that," said Pullen. "It was Electrifying Mojo; he played an important part in training the ear of the people of Detroit to listen to different things. They had fifteen-minute mixes of Devo, fifteen-minute mixes of Kraftwerk, and banging it into your head for seven days in a row. So we had no choice but to like it. The record companies now, if they were smart enough, they could do the same thing with this music that we're doing. It's always a pop phenomenon, pop culture that people - You - They want to hear it only because of the record companies just giving it to them like that. It's all about having the balls to push it to people to let them know that this is the new and exciting thing that's happening. This is the future, this is creativity, this is art, this music, at the end of the day."

The Bronx born, DJ Frankie Knuckles "The Godfather of House Music," came up as a fashion designer alongside his best friend, Larry Levan. Levan's experimental Disco meets Philly Soul DJ sets utilising synthesisers and drum machines, inside the legendary invite-only Paradise Garage, birthing New York House, Garage, and the contemporary club aesthetic. Knuckles relocated to Chicago in 1977, to play out his heady mix of Disco, Soul, Euro-Synth, and a dab of Rock at the members-only gay club, Warehouse. His 1983 purchase of a Roland TR-909 drum machine from Derrick May combining with a sampler and experimental live mixes inside The Power Plant club leading to the birth of Chicago House.

DJ Jesse Saunders integration of primary turntablism, accenting loops and repetition by stripping records to drum or bass culminating in the first House 12", "On & On," co-written with Vince Lawrence in 1983, and released in January 1984 on Jes Say Records.

DJ Chip E. producing records in 1984, also recognised as a "Godfather of House," released Jack Trax with Mirage featuring "It's House" and "Time to Jack" leading to revered terms "House" and "Jack".

Byron Stingily enjoying the Miami sunshine @ WMC 1997.

Chicago labels Trax Records and D.J. International Records issuing deep, hard, soulful, and Acid House classics by Adonis, Larry Heard, J.M. Silk, Frankie Knuckles, Marshall Jefferson, Farley "Jackmaster" Funk, Jesse Saunders, Shawn Christopher, and others.

Ten City was forming in 1987, becoming one of the first crews to drop vocals over House tracks. "Well, we tried to be," said Ten City vocalist Byron Stingily in our spring 1997 interview at the Miami Winter Music Conference.

"At the time when House first started, a lot of people in Chicago were doing tracks and things like that, a lot of sampled tracks, and at the time what we called Jack Trax. We felt, with our producer, Marshall Jefferson, me and him, the idea to - Ten City was gonna be a group of songs and about arrangements and things like that. We wanted to bring those elements to Dance Music, and it feels good to see that some of the songs are still able to get played in clubs, like "Devotion" and "Right Back," and "That's the Way." It feels good to look back ten years later because that's what we were striving for."

New York City Hardcore Punk, Moby released the seminal Rave classic alternate-mix of "Go" in March 1991. He spoke of being unable to differentiate Techno and House in our fall 1993 interview. "When House music happened it appealed to the same part of me that even hardcore had appealed because it's so subversive. It was this weird underground type thing. When Techno first started happening, I didn't know the difference between the two 'cause there were a lot of House records that were very Techno sounding, and a lot of House records, like Inner City, that was very House sounding. To me, there was no difference. I remember for about six months being completely confused as to what the distinctions were. Then I started making my records three years ago."

The differential state of mind between the two cities being Detroit artists primarily stood by each other as a united front, whereas Chicago artists more or less split up as individuals. Detroit's Stacey Pullen explained the reason why in his *Modulations: Cinema for the Ear* interview with Director Iara Lee.

Moby @ 318 Richmond St W, Toronto, 1992. Photo by Edmund Yee

"I agree, only because - how can I describe this? We're together only because when the riots happened in 1967, that brought togetherness into the city of Detroit. The city was in turmoil; we had riots, we had different types of cultural and racial barriers that plagued the city at the time. So basically now we're proteges of that environment that happened back in those days. And we know what it is to struggle for one another; we know what it is when it comes to succeeding and excellence. We know when we see another person amongst our peers doing the same thing, we push each other. We do music together sometimes; we run out of the same studios. It's one man helping the next man."

Kevin Saunderson addressed the holier than thou attitude of Detroit Techno purists in our 1992 interview. "I know it started out that way. I don't know. It seems everybody wants to follow Detroit or fake what we've done; it's still the equipment that's there. We try not to follow other people though. What Detroit is, is a city that creates very original music and that's the play for us. Where most people seem to follow us or they're followers, and we tend to be leaders whether it's popular or not. We do our own thing."

Overseas, 808 State formed in 1987, taking their name from the Roland TR-808, becoming the first Manchester group to play Acid House by paying homage to Chicago Jack Trax and Transmat Records. "This whole scene now that people are calling Rave, that's what it was born out of," said 808 State's Darren Partington in our summer 1993 interview. "And before that, it was the Hi-NRG in the early 70's, the gay scene, which nobody ever talks about."

"Theme From S'Express" by S'Express topped the UK Singles Charts for two weeks in 1988. A Guy Called Gerald, a founding member of 808 State, releasing the Acid House classic, "Voodoo Ray," in 1989, reaching number 12 on the UK Singles Chart. Adamski's "Killer," featuring Seal, hitting number one on the UK Singles Chart for four weeks in May and June 1990.

Karl Hyde and Rick Smith of Greater London band Underworld began to work on a fresh hybrid sound with new member Darren Emmerson, following their tour of America supporting Eurythmics, in "a formative stumbling way" in 1990.

By blending the guitar-oriented funky electro-pop of their early records and turning what was once a five-piece band into a Techno-rock fusion. "We had thrown away a lot of stuff that was attempting to fuse together these things that we had in our head," said Karl Hyde in our 1996 interview. "And so it was a very deliberate move towards a fusion."

The January 1994 release of the renowned *dubnobasswithmyheadman* album realising the transition from synth pop to Techno and Progressive House.

Karl Hyde

Rick Smith

Darren Emmerson

Armand Van Helden

Cajmere/Green Velvet

Boo Williams

Paul Johnson
DJ Funk
DJ Sneak
DJ Rush
Wax Master
Hyperactive
Jammin Gerald
Brian Wilson
George Clinton
Lil Louis
Ashley Beedle
Neil Landstrumm
Kenny Dope
DJ Hell
Louie Vega
K-Alexi
Dr. Dre is in the house, yeah
Armando in the house
Gemini is in the house
Jeff Mills in the house
DJ Dee-on

DJ Milton
DJ Slugo
DJs on the low
Green Velvet
Joey Beltram
DJ ESP
Roy Davis
Boo Williams
DJ Tonka
DJ Skull
DJ Pierre
Mike Dearborn in the house, yeah

Todd Edwards in the house
Romanthony in the house
CVO in the house
Luke Slater
Derrick Carter
Robert Hood
Parris Mitchess
Dave Clarke is in the house
Van Helden in the house
Armani in the house
Surgeon is in the house, yeah

Daft Punk *"Teachers"* (1997)

Derrick Carter

The alternative post-punk world that led Thomas Bangalter and Guy-Manuel de Homem-Christo to Darlin' had lost its shine. The records were still fresh. However, they were nowhere near as exciting as the rise, culture, and allure of underground dance music. Indeed, the timing of the Daft Punk sound revolution could not be better. By the summer of 1993, Daft Punk was psyched up and ready to take on the world, and nothing would stop them. Out of respect and admiration, they went straight to Richie Hawtin. Sadly, he declined. It was all a dream.

Bangalter and de Homem-Christo attended the massive Dance Europe Weekender, *eurodisney*, near Euro Disneyland east of Paris, September 24, 25, 26, 1993. The event featuring DJ sets by Sasha, Tony Humphries, Paul Oakenfold, Andrew Weatherall, Graeme Park, Pete Tong, Laurent Garnier, Sven Vath, and others, and live performances from Inner City, The Reese Project, and M. People. Demo tape in hand, they met Scottish DJ and producer, Stuart McMillan of Slam, co-founder of Soma Quality Recordings.

Daft Punk was bringing in their new groove beginning with the limited release of "The New Wave"/"Assault" EP in April 1994, on Soma. The original "Da Funk"/"Rollin' N Scratchin'" following on Soma in May 1995. Thomas Bangalter branched off to start the Roulé label in 1995, managed by Gildas Loaëc (co-creator of Kitsuné), releasing the five-song solo EP, **Trax On Da Rocks**. The early Soma and Roulé releases borrowing heavily from the sounds of Chicago's Cajmere/Green Velvet and DJ Sneak, and New York City's Roger Sanchez. Blurring the distinction between House and Techno by embodying progressive elements of Funk and Breaks through the filtered loops of a stripped down vintage danceable electro.

Daft Punk's sprint towards success sparking in 1996. The two-part "Indo Silver Club" 12" coming in February 1996, released by Soma Quality Recordings. Bangalter was dropping the "Spinal Scratch"/"Spinal Beats" 12" on Roulé soon after. Bangalter and de Homem-Christo marking their first overseas booking at the *Even Further* outdoor festival and camp-out over a soggy Wisconsin Memorial Day long weekend.

The critical provocateur: DJ, club promoter, and law student, Pedro Winter. Winter was beginning to manage the duo, savvily negotiating a licensing deal with Virgin Records to release albums through its production company, Daft Trax. Daft Punk was becoming the first group signed to a major label with a home studio recording.

Daft Punk had experienced a shade of international success and buzz with underground releases on Soma. Still, Virgin Records were designating the first album, *Homework*, global priority opening

the floodgates for a big budget video paving the way for the Spike Jonze directed "Da Funk," subtitled *Big City Nights*. The tale of anthropomorphic dog Charles, in a leg cast and crutches, carrying a Ghetto-blaster while trying to find his way in the big city. Bangalter and de Homem-Christo cleverly absent. A crowning achievement is ending the year breaking down pre-existing electronic music barriers.

Dance Music at its highest level since the Disco Explosion. The Prodigy and Chemical Brothers charging into North America at the juncture of a digital revolution. Marketing monkeys were rushing to direct media, retail, and consumers to the next big thing, neatly typifying, itemising, and pigeonholing Dance Music as Corn Flakes in a bullshit Electronica box. Nevertheless, to the dismay of longstanding underground purists, punters began flocking in with money in hand, in record numbers.

The debut Daft Punk album, *Homework*, arriving in January 1997, is both a satisfying homage to the artists and producers who influenced the duo and a nod to the period spent completing the collection in their home studio. The high derivative of the 60s and 70 artistic approaches of Bangalter and de Homem-Christo to conceal their identities adding to the intrigue and surrounding buzz. A response to the minimal music and imagery that dominated the 90's, visuals and artwork as a means to exact others to join in. There was no desire to be pop stars, rock stars, or the precursor to today's superstar DJ. Cool music, people dancing and enjoying *Homework* was the goal.

The release of *Homework's* second single, "Around The World," came March 17, 1997. Five days later, Daft Punk marked their second trip to North America to attend the *Winter Music Conference* in South Beach, Miami, Florida, March 22-26, 1997. WMC being the conclave every genre of the international dance music industry convenes each year, to advance the platform as one. Its delegates, artists, DJs, labels, booking agents, club owners, and core constituents of every city attending seminars, workshops, day and night events, and revelling in the Florida sunshine.

Come into my Planet Soul @ WMC 1997.

I reached out to Russell Hergert, Virgin Records Canada Marketing Representative, and negotiated an exclusive Daft Punk cover story interview at the *Winter Music Conference*. Though, I was flown to Miami and registered for the conference by Quality Music & Video, who were flourishing on the back of mail order products Sweepa rubber broom and charismatic Hockey icon *Don Cherry's Rock'Em Sock'Em Hockey* video series of hockey fights.

Quality is known to produce and air an endless stream of nationally televised infomercials to stimulate sales, the big spend, high yield marketing stance spilt over to its music department.

Naturally, Quality checked me into the iconic luxury Fontainebleau Hotel on South Beach. The host Hotel of Winter Music Conference, it served as ground zero to critical members of the international dance music community and conference delegates. WMC patrons were taking over the sprawling property, dominating its lobby, pool area and bar. A veritable trainspotters paradise. A walk to the pool intersected by superstar DJs, promoters, club owners, industry insiders, and hangers-on.

Quality Music set up a few random interviews to promote artists signed to partner labels and songs licensed for compilations. The first offering, UK House artists, Sol Brothers. I was up in one of the Fontainebleau towers speaking with Planet Soul producer and Miami DJ, George Acosta, when Quality summoned me to interview Nadine Renee and her producer, the legendary Arthur Baker. Renee had recorded the international hit "Set U Free" with Acosta and fronted Planet Soul before an acrimonious split. My extended conversation with Acosta was leaving her and Baker waiting. Baker was offering his best fuck you hand over face pose post interview.

I added to the coverage of the Conference by spotting and asking artists to talk. Chicago Deep House vocal legend, Byron Stingily graciously taking time out for an interview and casual photo by the pool. Invitations to sponsored daytime events taking place offsite at boutique hotels and spread along Collins Ave, Washington Ave, and the scenic Ocean Drive boardwalk. Leading to time capsule photos of Danny Tenaglia, David Morales and Maurice Joshua, Erick "More" Morillo, Jellybean Benitez, Braxton Holmes and DJ Sneak, Juan Atkins and Eddie "Flashin'" Fowlkes, and Armand Van Helden, Junior Sanchez, and Strictly Rhythm A&R prophet, Gladys Pizarro, by the pool. Evenings yielding exclusive small venue DJ sets and large club parties by the world's top DJs, and multiple Cuban dinners at Puerto Sagua.

The undeniable highlight of the Conference, Masters At Work *Nuyorican Soul Fiesta* at The Shore Club, Monday, March 24, 1997. MCA Records Canada was connecting me in advance to the President of GRP Records, distributor of Giant Step, resulting in landing side-stage for perhaps the most magnificent live performance I ever witnessed. "Little" Louie Vega and Kenny "Dope" Gonzalez jamming a live performance of the essential *Nuyorican Soul* album featuring Jocelyn Brown, La India, Roy Ayers, percussionists Tito Puente Jr. and Luis Quintero Jr., an excellent selection of Miami musicians, and Roni Size. Poolside Cuban food, cigar rollers, volleyball, and short post-show interviews with Ayers, Vega, and La India.

The unforgettable Gavin Gerbz, Eddy K and Marc "DJ Peoples" Vane boat cruise, featuring S-Men - Roger Sanchez, DJ Sneak and Junior Sanchez. A showcase of Toronto's debaucherous Industry nightclub lifestyle on exhibit for a chosen few international massive and heads. Dangerous to the point even the Captain jumped on the dance-floor and took a wine as his boat cruised the Miami harbour. The cruise was living on in infamy as select footage aired on the BBC.

Daft Punk was spending time promoting *Homework* in a limited number of interviews. Bonding and solidifying the Mongoloids brotherhood. Regrettably experiencing gloom as the plan to arm Teachers with promotional vinyl was snuffed out by an unknown assailant who managed to haul off the entire stack, gutting Bangalter, de Homem-Christo and crew. Undoubtedly, a draft punky thrashing.

The designated time of my interview arriving in the mid-afternoon, Sunday, March 23, 1997. Thomas, Guy-Manuel and I were greeting each other for the first time. Responding to questions concerning "Da Funk" dog, anonymity, dance music, the creation process, remixes, and the immediate future. Bangalter was doing most of the speaking, de Homem-Christo limiting himself to few words.

Post-interview, long before "Robot Rock" and iconic helmets, each placing a Daft Punk promotional sticker over eyes to maintain anonymity. I shot one frame, waved goodbye, and left the room heading back to the pool area for a cocktail. WMC '97, indeed a whirlwind of unforgettable activity and music.

La India

Nuyorican Soul Fiesta

Roy Ayers

Two weeks later, April 12, 1997, Daft Punk made their Canadian debut, playing a DJ set selecting from three-hundred records at Toronto's Industry Nightclub to a roomful of core heads, along with special guest from Chicago DJ Sneak, and Mario J. The worst designed cover of *Peace! Magazine* history, featuring two Daft Punk slides, is issued the next month. The duo was enacting the summer legs of the *Daftendirektour* in North America and the European festival circuit. Daft Punk was arriving back in Toronto to perform a spectacular show inside Toronto's RPM Warehouse, September 1, 1997. Guy-Manuel de Homem-Christo spotted in front of the venue post-show eating local street meat.

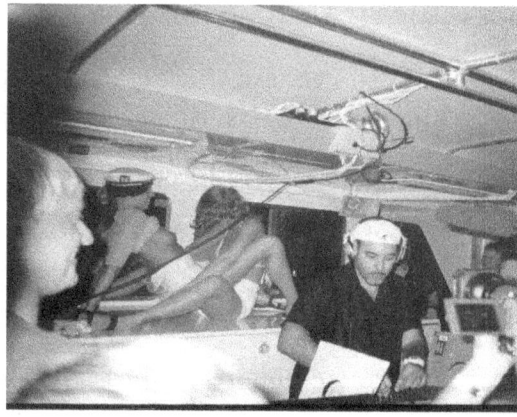

WMC 1997 boat cruise!

Guy-Manuel de Homem-Christo digging in the crates the crates @ Industry, April 12, 1997.

The third *Homework* single, "Burnin'" was released on September 15, 1997. Its filmed in Chicago concept-driven multi-media video paving the way for what would follow in years to come. Mongoloids Roger Sanchez, DJ Sneak, Junior Sanchez, and Industry's Gavin Bryan in the hotel ballroom evacuation scene.

Roulé released Alan Braxe's French Disco filtered "Vertigo" with its Bangalter and Braxe "(Virgo Edit)" in October 1997. De Homem-Christo was capping the year kickstarting his label, Crydamoure, with partner Éric Chedeville, AKA Rico The Wizard. Its debut single as Le Knight Club, "Santa Claus"/"Holidays On Ice." Daft Punk wrapping up the *Daftendirektour* with December shows in Los Angeles and Berlin. Its singles and remixes a presence on the charts and in the clubs, *Homework* was selling upwards of one million copies worldwide.

The fourth and final single off *Homework*, "Revolution 909," was issued February 16, 1998. The video directed by Roman Coppola, the son of Francis Ford Coppola and brother to Sofia Coppola, portrays the French government's anti-party Police clampdown. Thomas Bangalter and Guy-Manuel de Homem-Christo returning to North America in March to attend the Miami *Winter Music Conference* and hang out with Mongoloid brothers.

Have you ever heard the behind the music tale of "Music Sounds Better With You"? Allegedly, Virgin Records UK laid claim to being responsible for the success of Daft Punk, making the music a distant second. Somehow, someway, in the pre-social media snail mail world, word leaked back to the Daft Punk camp leaving them disappointed and disrespected.

Ealy in the summer of 1998, Stardust is born. Thomas Bangalter, Alan Braxe, and vocalist Benjamin Diamond jammed what became "Music Sounds Better With You," live inside the Rex Club, Paris.

Entering Bangalter's Daft House home studio the next day to record the song. A sample of Chaka Khan's "Fate" the whipped cream and cherry. Roulé 305, one of the greatest dance music songs of all-time, coming July 20, 1998. Among the highest selling singles of the year in the UK, topping the US Billboard Dance Club Songs chart for two weeks. The five-song *Trax on Da Rocks Vol. 2*, also on Roulé, coming October 1998. Payback's A Mutha, ask King Tee.

When DJ Sneak moved from Chicago to Toronto, Industry Nightclub had the plug to the international DJ community. In celebration of his 29th birthday, **Boomer Brothers Presents DJ Sneak's Birthday Beats**, November 5th, 1998. The Thursday night event discreetly promoted to those in the know and attended by 850 patrons, featuring a line-up for the ages: Thomas Bangalter was flying overseas to throw down a four-turntable, two-mixer set with Sneak. Toronto favourite, the luminary Derrick Carter was closing out the night. Doc Martin, unannounced taking over for Bangalter and joining Sneak for a surprise four-table set. Junior Sanchez, King Britt, Bear Who?, and Sneak's brother, Kaiser Soze pushing the vibes.

"We wanted to do something special for Sneak's birthday," recalls Industry co-owner, Gavin Bryan. "I called Pedro (Winter) to see if Thomas would be interested in coming over to surprise him. The event was on a Thursday night and had the energy of a Saturday night rager. It was the perfect getaway for Thomas as people were straight up bootlegging "Music Sounds Better With You" all over the world, due to its massive success. Sadly, "friends" in the game were letting him down as well. We decided on a spontaneous four day trip to Jamaica after the surprise birthday party at Industry. Thomas needed to get away from Europe, and we bonded during that Toronto /Jamaica trip."

Bangalter flew to Jamaica with Toronto residents Rory Levy (Boomer Brothers), Matt C (Industry), and Gavin Bryan, spending four nights on the seven-mile beach of Negril, Jamaica. (Fast forward to 2007, Daft Punk selected Rory Levy to manage and sell **Alive 2007** tour merchandise, the only non-Parisian in the crew).

Daft Punk returned to the Miami *Winter Music Conference* playing a rare DJ set inside the Cameo Theatre, March 13, 1999.

Flying to Toronto to join DJ Sneak, Josh Wink and more, for their only other DJ set of the year, September 4, 1999, with over eight thousand people inside the 200 000 sq ft Toronto Congress Centre. Bangalter, Pedro Winter, de Homem-Christo and The Wizard spendng a few days in the City after the show. Winter as DJ Chavez DJing a Tuesday night set on the BamBoo rooftop patio.

Thomas Bangalter, Gavin Gerbz & Pedro Winter

Music's got me feeling so free.
We're gonna celebrate.
Celebrate and dance so free.
One more time.

Papa Cyril Bryan & "The Wizard"!

"One More Time" surfaced November 13, 2000. At one fell swoop, it's infectious heartbeat, and Romanthony vocals lit up clubs and radio worldwide. Topping the charts of France, Canada, and Scotland, and the Dance Charts of UK, and Billboard's Dance Club Songs and Hot Dance Singles Sales. Destined to be voted number one dance song of all-time by *Mixmag* readers in 2010.

Pedro Winter, Eric "The Wizard" Chevdeville, The Original Kid Rock, Thomas Bangalter, Gavin Gerbz, Stephen Riff.

DJ Chavez @ BamBoom, September 4, 1999.

The release of *Discovery* around the corner, Virgin Records Canada flew us to New York City, January 2001, for an exclusive cover feature. Steve Carty was booked to shoot. I contacted Raphie Aronowitz of Ecko Unltd., who supplied crucial pieces of Ecko's upcoming brand, Physical Science. PSY SCI, a unique new line representing current technology, authentic design and functional integrity. The secret identity and background of the particular guest interviewer withheld. Genuine love and insight of House music, and confidence within the Daft Punk camp.

We met Thomas Bangalter, Guy-Manuel de Homem-Christo, and Pedro Winter at a Manhattan studio loft. Levels from the standard hotel room, unmade bed and promo stickers of March 1997. Carty was setting up his equipment as the special mystery guest and I recorded Daft Punk. Bangalter and de Homem-Christo examining success, *Discovery*, the state of House music, the influence of Hip-Hop, and much more. Post-interview, an unveiling of the now iconic robot helmets and gloves. (Unfortunately, someone failed to inform us of the opportunity to send a message for Daft Punk to program the helmets in advance).

Discovery was issued February 26, 2001. Life is never the same.

Part One: The Shit

(South Beach, Miami, Florida)

It is March 1997; Virgin Records is rolling out Daft Punk to the international media at the *Winter Music Conference*. Thomas Bangalter and Guy-Manuel de Homem-Christo are happy to be present amongst Teachers and peers. Touched by the universally positive response to *Homework*, and "Da Funk" reaching number one on the Billboard US Dance Club Songs chart.

The designated interview room is basic, indeed no suite. Bangalter and de Homem-Christo laid back and comfortable in t-shirts and sneakers. Greetings exchanged, they move to sit on the edge of the unmade double-bed, as I take the chair to face. Voice IDs requested to get the quotes correct.

"My name is Thomas."

"My name is Guy-Manuel."

Everybody is on Daft Punk. Everyone is saying Daft Punk is the shit. Why?

"I don't know," responded Thomas Bangalter. "We don't realise that much that when we are in Paris. We're more staying in France, so it's really surprising to get there in the States, and everybody is after you and saying that they like the record. The only thing that we can say is that we're excited, and it's a very satisfying thing to see that a lot of people that have influenced us, a lot of producers and stuff, we meet them and they like our stuff too, which is a feedback thing, which is cool."

The positive emotions elicited by Daft Punk's music holding weight. A rare understanding and interconnection of rhythmic House and Techno driving people to release energy.

When do you know the music works and is the shit?

"Maybe when you're finishing a track," explained Guy-Manuel de Homem-Christo. "Maybe you know it's going to be danceable."

"We more or less when we do the track trying to get to some point," continued Thomas Bangalter. "When we are starting the track and just with the rhythms and so, adding stuff - Should we do that or that. Maybe at one point, we say, 'Okay, that's it.' That's when the track is quite simple and stuff; we don't have that much, and say, 'Yeah, that's okay to dance.' After that, we more hesitating and putting the album on the heart and asking yourself the question. But, while we finish the track, once we are quite confident with it at some point."

The album is called *Homework*. Did you consciously go in to pay tribute to the people you grew up hearing?

"Maybe we consciously go and trying to finish the album; it was like people were asking for it. Some people were waiting for it," explained Bangalter. "We quite lazy, so we said, 'Okay, we got to do our homework,' and went to our little home studio and finished the thing. But after that, it's just a concept as it could have been another one. We thought it would be cool, be funnier not to do like we've always - computer-generated stuff or futuristic stuff. This music could fit with also more vintage images and stuff rather than just the whole visual - new visuals that are always a bit the same."

Sadly, the beloved premise of *Homework* existing as a tribute to those who influenced Bangalter and de Homem-Christo shattered with a subtle reality.

There is a lot of imagery in the music.

"Yeah," agreed de Homem-Christo.

"It's funny to play with," said Bangalter. " That's probably maybe not a Rock thing, but from the 60s and the 70s there has been a lot of imagery in music, and the music being more minimal in the 90's. The media imagery has become more or less minimal, which is a bad thing because even with very, very minimal music, you could do cool visuals and stuff, and artwork. It was maybe a way to show and to interest people to do so, to work more. Today, there's lots of cool music, but sometimes the artwork and stuff are not enough considered to be important."

You're kicking the funky masks.

"Yeah," said Bangalter. "It's a way to - We don't want to be pop stars, or Rockstars and House stars, whatever. We wanted to make cool music and make people dance, and people like the album and so on. It's not about being ourselves or whatever. It's about maybe playing live, maybe making people dance and that's it, and having living with that."

The essence of Bangalter's words helps to uncover variables of the equation that compels the duo to maintain anonymity. The yin and yang of Virgin Records running collateral campaigns, and the pair refusing to play a part in the filthy lucre often associated with success.

Here you are an international priority for Virgin Records, but you want to retain your anonymity.

"Yeah!" agreed Bangalter. "This is it, but what I say is maybe it's inevitable to become more or less the thing, to become more or less very famous and the star thing, but maybe the logo is more the star. I'm saying, where you see the logo everywhere. In New York, there are lots of posters, and here there's lots of stickers, posters, and stuff, so it's becoming more or less very, very big. But at least as part of the promotional thing, it's not our face. We don't want us to be the star. If it is the music gets more and more popular and if people love it, then eventually, Daft Punk, in itself, will be maybe a star thing, and then, maybe. But not doing the dumb thing and as an ego thing, and we can make things, push the music forward. This is not at all something that we want to take personally."

Enter Charles, the anthropomorphic dog of "Da Funk" video, assumed by many a member of Daft Punk in costume. The favourite Spike Jonze directed video inciting passionate debate as to its high-concept meaning.

My favourite question people ask me about Daft Punk, and it is funny because it's ridiculous, which one of you is the dog?

"It's none," responded Guy-Manuel de Homem-Christo.

That is what is weird because you're in the limelight and people think you're some dog-guy.

"Yeah," laughed Bangalter. "A lot of people know that Daft Punk is one guy; it's a dog."

Guy-Manuel de Homem-Christo is a man of few words.

Do you do any talking?

"Not so much," replied de Homem-Christo.

Daft Punk emerged as somewhat of an enigma to those unaware of their independent output on Soma Quality Recordings before "Da Funk," *Homework*, and "Around The World." A handful of singles and remixes to their credit. "Chord Memory for Mongoloid brother Ian Pooley and "Disco Cubizm for Parisian I: Cube are the standouts, though some may argue "Life Is Sweet" for Chemical Brothers.

Let's talk remixes. You did one for the Chemical Brothers. What are you working on now?

"Now, apart from doing interviews, we're more working on, not on remixes or new stuff, but the live thing that we'll be preparing and that will be hitting Europe starting June or July," said Bangalter. "And then doing more festival stuff and more gigs later in the year. It's all about preparing the set up for the studios and for the live thing, so it's not at all about recording natural. But trying to do new stuff live also, and so musically that's what we're doing right now. What we're focusing and looking forward, to going into parties and play live, which is good to meet people."

The night before the interview, Bangalter and de Homem-Christo played a DJ set inside a small Miami lounge that was attended by a handful of those in the know, including Mongoloids brothers. (The date and venue unlisted on any Daft Punk associated sites).

So last night was not your show? You were dropping wax, and that's it. Word is you freak it when you play live with samplers.

"No. This is maybe a misunderstanding," said Bangalter. "What we're doing here now is more a DJ thing, just playing some records into some clubs. The thing with last night, it was not a club. People were staring, and actually, the sound was not good, so it wouldn't be cool to dance or stay. But eventually, we'll find some good clubs in this city and play."

Set to play live further in the year on the soon to be titled *Daftendirektour*, Bangalter confirmed the upcoming stop inside Toronto's Industry Nightclub, April 12, would also be a DJ set with no samplers.

As a self-contained unit, Daft Punk wrote, produced, and mixed themselves at the Daft House home studio. Signing with Virgin Records opening the doors to a remix budget. Armand Van Helden was the first remixer to put hands on their music with his "Ten Minutes of Funk" Mix of "Da Funk."

As remixers, how does it feel when you hand over a track to a remixer, such as the Armand Van Helden scenario?

"It feels funny," said Bangalter. "We're not quite used to that because maybe some people, even in the underground stuff, since the way they started they had lots of people remixing their shit and stuff, but it's the first time. This year is the first time we're being remixed, so it's quite a new feel, but it depends if we like the remix then we happy, and if not, then we say, 'Okay.' So, as we like the Armand Van Helden remix, we think it's funny because obviously, it's not our track, but it's our name, whatever, so it's a funny thing."

Europe's penchant for electronic derived pop music opened the gate for American House and Techno to creep in. Bored with the wholesale club aesthetic, a new breed of promoters began to hold massive underground parties in fields, warehouses and aeroplane hangars. A co-opting of space made for transformative possibilities fueled by a communion based on the music, peace, love, unity and respect, and the drug ecstasy. Non-stop instrumental music, pulsating bass and repetitive beats bare of visible musicians. Out of control bodies dancing in a trance, resulting in a government crackdown.

From what I read, the politics in France is fucked up.

Thomas Bangalter, "Yeah."

How is it to work as an artist in a community like that?

"Working as an artist or making music is okay. There's no problem with that," responded Bangalter. "At least the freedom of just expression is okay, but it's more the party, the whole party thing if you are working as a promoter or whatever. You've got the clubs that are in Paris or outside, and it's okay to do stuff in those clubs, but you can not do any more one-off spots here, Raves, for now, because the police and the government are always trying to avoid that. Making a big confusion with taking our Devil music, repetitive thing and drugs, and think everything is bad and young gatherings and stuff. So, it's really bad now but eventually with the music being more - The music is not taken very seriously still. It's like 'Yeah, you're cheesy dance stuff,' and eventually if what we're doing or what other people are doing is being more or less considered outside, then people speak about it and say it's good and stuff. Maybe people will more consider it music in a new better way, and maybe we'll be more able to party."

With "Da Funk" crossing over to mainstream and the emergence of electronic music in pop culture, many began to listen to this exciting "new music" for the first time. It was the dawn of producers and songwriters growth from melody and lyrics to tracks and hooks.

For someone to get the Daft Punk vibe, do they have to do homework first?

"I don't know," said Bangalter. "I don't know. Probably they have to be acting and being creative rather than doing nothing, but I don't know."

To get Daft Punk, do they have to be exposed to the music previously? Can you come in and take over the Nirvana fans?

"I think you don't have to do your homework, maybe," continued Bangalter. "We not purists ourselves. We don't have five-thousand electro records or five-thousand disco records at home, so it's not like 'Yeah, we know that.' We not 'Yeah, we were there in '88 and stuff.' We discovered that in '92, so the thing is we just - All we are showing is that it's okay if you discovered this music today. Don't be ashamed and stuff because I can't stand these people who say 'What! You don't know that!' And being snobby. The underground people have some efforts to make too if they fight for that kind of music. Every day someone is turning into it now. It's one more guy who is liking it, and that's a good point. So, if somebody who likes, who has never listened to any House or dance music and even who hated House music, now, if he's into it, that's a good thing, because they'll be more and more people into it.

What's next for Daft Punk?

"Ahh, another interview, I guess," said Bangalter.

You got to say something.

Thomas Bangalter whispered to Guy-Manuel de Homem-Christo, "Something. "Something," said de Homem-Christo to end the interview.

I asked the duo to pose for a casual photo. Bangalter and de Homem-Christo reached for promotional stickers of the Daft Punk logo and each fixed one over their eyes, turned to face the camera, and smiled. I shot one frame, thanked them, and headed back to the Fontainebleau pool area.

Daft Punk spent the remainder of the season doing a handful of interviews and preparing to hit the road. The 1997 *Daftendirektour* was playing summer European festivals, September North American theatre and club dates, and fall European shows, ending in Berlin, December 20, 1997. Bangalter and de Homem-Christo playing cool music, getting feedback, meeting and making new friends in every country.

THE REAL DJ SNEAK

DJ Sneak is a vital component of the second generation of Chicago House producers and DJs. Known for his masterful ability to run any disco song through filtered loops and get dance floors popping. And the third shout-out of Daft Punk's "Teachers."

The significance of his early barrage of releases for Cajual, Defiant, Relief, Jinxx, Strictly Rhythm, Henry Street Music and others, notably "Groovadelic" and "Sneak's A Freak" clearly ascribed on "Burnin'," which he remixed for Daft Punk, appearing in its video. Moving on to collaborate with Guy-Manuel de Homem-Christo and Rico The Wizard on "Intergalaktic Disko" in 1997, and "Think Love, Not Hate" released in 1999, and writing the lyrics for "Digital Love," the third single off *Discovery*.

Sneak's roots go back to the graffiti scene where he learned to become adept at airbrushing clothing. Beginning to DJ house parties and work in a record store, to earn a discount, at the dawn of the Chicago House era in 1984, when he was dubbed Sneak.

"I sneak music when I'm playing," he told me in our summer 1997 interview. "I play certain cuts that people are into, introduce a lot of new music. I like to break a lot of the new records and new artists, stuff like that. I'm always hip and getting promos and stuff like that, so I go in there and do my thing."

He bought his first drum machine in 1992 and negotiated a sampler with an indie label in exchange for music under a different name. "You got to start somewhere," he said. Music taking over, he began to produce records and arrived at his sound based on crowd reactions to live mixes.

"I work hard, man, seriously. In the summer of 1994, I told four of my best friends and my brother that I was gonna be somebody big and I wanted to make it, and I was gonna do it. Knowing the stuff through retail, I got to know a lot of distributors and important people in the music industry. They gave me the shortcut to where I'm at today. The last year and a half have been great. The last three years for me has been the greatest years of my life, so far. I've travelled all over and played for a lot of important people, for regular people, or forty people, or ten thousand people. I've played as much to a room with ten thousand people in there. That's like stage fright but not really 'cause I do what I do. The one thing that helped me out with all that was the records. I had the fever. I had the bug, and all I would do is - this is funny 'cause I always say this - I get stoned and do tracks!"

Sneak's unusual sound is incomparable to New York producers. By experimenting with different bass and drums, he generated new music utilising old refried disco and distinct accents earning international respect.

"There's a way that I've earned the respect that if I get the Disco record I know, I can make a track out of it. I don't care what Disco record, even it's some cheesy shit; I'll find something and make it a whole track and build around that. The records are made for people in the club. Usually, you could be at home studying, you could be at home writing, you could be at home doing dishes, and you could pop a tape of DJ Sneak, and you'll enjoy it. The music that I make is for people like me, and people like to chill."

At the time of our 1997 interview, Sneak was preparing to release the third instalment of his acclaimed *Polyester* series, *Polyester 3*. Unfortunately, he had experienced an issue with a sample of the 1983 Paul Simpson instrumental remix of Montana Orchestra's "It Looks Like Love," and had to pull a song off **Polyester 2**.

"*Polyester 3*, I'm excited. It's cool. The tracks are up to date. I'm waiting to come out, seriously. Tracks are Sneak with a little bit of Da Mongoloid, Daft Punk, Armand, everybody's feeling into it, and my feel.   The last year I've been hanging with some of the top producers that are young like Daft Punk and Armand and Roger, a lot of people like that, Junior Sanchez. We feed off each other's stuff. It's a combination of that. I'm trying to work on a lot of music now but not having a lot of time actually 'cause of all the gigs and stuff like that.

Busy on the remix and production front and ready for the day, Sneak had the high-grade "You Can't Hide From Your Bud" in the can for Derrick Carter's UK based Classic label with plans for its North American release on his Defiant label swapping in a "U" for "You."

"As I was breaking into the whole producer thing I was finding out how record labels were, and I didn't agree with a lot of them, so I said, they're fucking up. I'll spend all the life savings I got, which at the moment I only had $2000 in the bank, and I put all my money into this one record, and I made my money back, so from then on, I planned out. It's been a while since Defiant had a record. Right now, Defiant is gonna have "Special K," which is a record I did, and it has Unabomber, the guys from here. Vince Ailey and Mario J and I did a mix for it, and That Kid Chris did a mix for me for that too, and then the other two mixes are mine. The "U Can't Hide From Your Bud" is gonna be released on Defiant too with Roger Sanchez remixes. There's a lot of stuff there I have made. I have some stuff coming out."

Excited for the possibilities of *Polyester 3*, Sneak had also completed "a favour remix for not a lot of money," for Backstreet Boys "*Quit Playing Games,*" *Sneak's Hardsteppin' Mongoloid Mix*. "I'm happy with it. I don't want people to think I'm making Backstreet Boys type of tracks 'cause I'm not, but it's fun remixing other people's stuff. It's bound to happen. Right now, I finished two Sneaker Pimp remixes for two different singles. I'm doing a remix for Daft Punk for "Burnin'" for Virgin. I'm also doing a remix of King Britt for Ovum, Columbia. I remixed some stuff for Wild Child. This one called "Come Bad Boy." Wild Child is a producer from London, England that passed away. There's some stuff coming out, man. I'm having fun remixing stuff, but I don't want to focus on that. I want to focus on making the original stuff 'cause that's what I'm used too."

DJ Sneak fell in love with the City of Toronto in the mid-90s, saw the fewcha and planned to seise the day by moving to the City in 1998. Heads were excited. His commanding presence, machismo, joie de vivre and ever-present spliff thrusting Toronto to the forefront of the new movement. He pursued business interests with Industry Nightclub, Unabomber Records, spent time with his girlfriend, and operated a record store to introduce new music.

"I like the city so much that I do a lot more for this city than I do for Chicago, to tell you the truth. In Chicago, stuff is tricky. You don't even know if it can work. Here, it's untouched ground, and I can do stuff."

By the time of his 29th birthday in November 1998, Sneak became firmly entrenched in the Toronto scene hosting and promoting regular events, and boosted the flavour of the city to Mongoloid brothers and beyond. *Boomer Brothers Presents DJ Sneak's Birthday Beats*, November 5, 1998, the stuff of legend. Multiple sites still offering a recording of the Sneak and Thomas Bangalter four-turntable, two-mixer set, however, listing it as the 1997 Industry DJ set of Daft Punk.

Toronto's place within the hierarchy of international dance music raised to the next level, a space it continues to occupy to this day. Sneak enduring in the city, eventually planting roots with his wife and starting a family, relocating to the warmer climate of Los Angeles, California, in 2017.

Thomas Bangalter and DJ Sneak in his "Smokey Mon" t-shirt @ WMC 2000.

BOOMER BROTHERS PRESENT SNEAK'S BIRTHDAY BEATS

Thomas Bangalter and DJ Sneak begin the beatdown. Nathan Barato sits for class.

Time for "Paris Angels."

Sneaking in the mix.

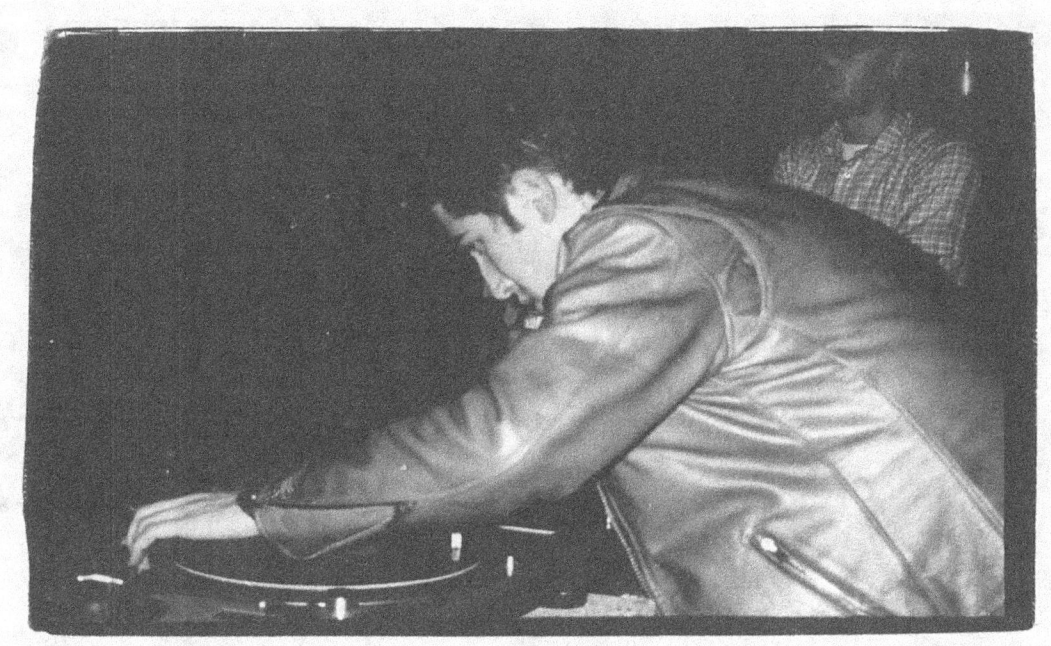

Thomas Bangalter laser focus on the mix prepares to drop "Music Sounds Better With You."

Bangalter x Unabmber Mario J

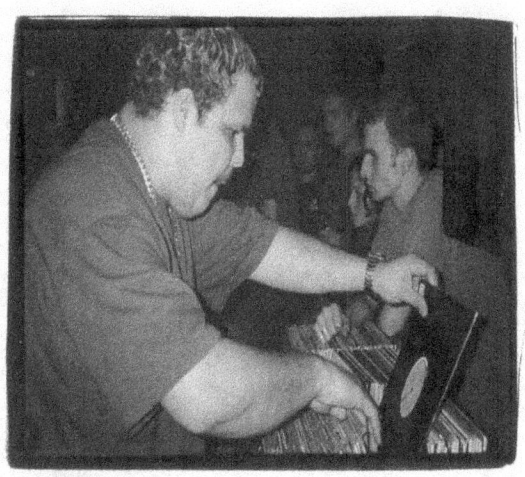

Looking for the Perfect Beat.

Digging in the crates

Armed and ready to drop "Buffalo Bunch."

Juan Sosa is Kaiser Soze.

Bangalter deep in the mix as Sneak reads a birthday card.

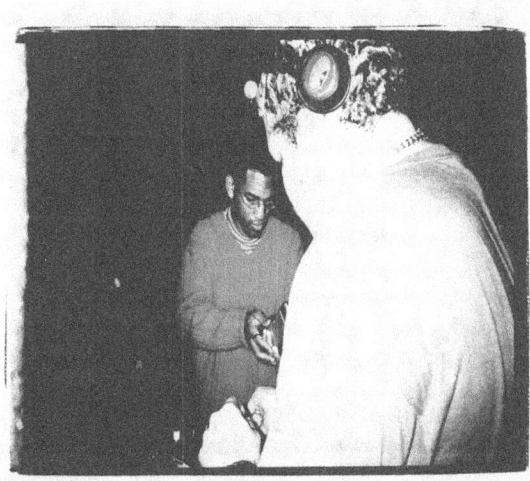

Down with the King.

Mecca and the Soul Brother.

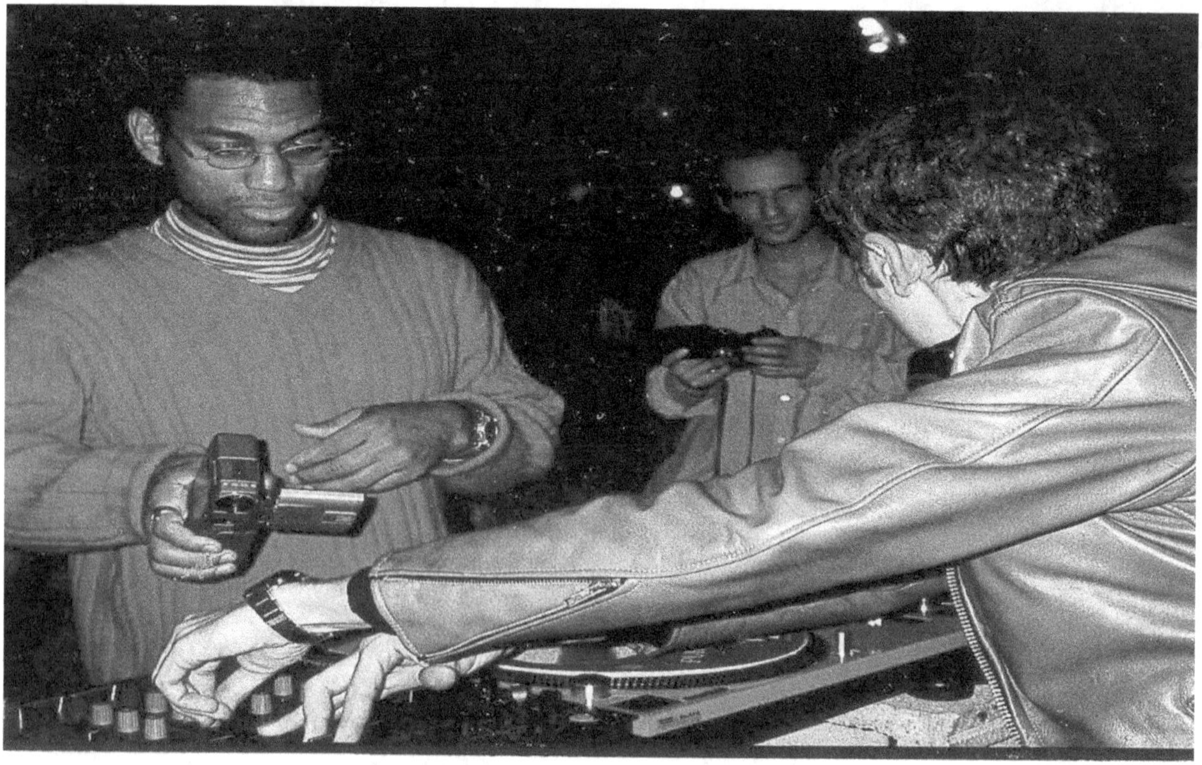

When will King Britt pull this footage from storage?

Russell Hergert x Thomas Bangalter.

Post beatdown drinks.

Unannounced four-turntable, two-mixer Doc Martin x Sneak magic.

Junior Sanchez, Gavin Gerbz, Paul "Soulgrabber" Jacobs & Sneak.

Industry's Colonel Matt C, King Britt, Gerbz & Junior Sanchez.

THE HISTORY OF DA MONGOLOIDS

Tales of Da Mongoloids have circulated for over twenty years. Whispers of a legendary crew of elite dance music producers sharing a mystical bond of brotherhood.

Who are its members? What did they have in common? Where did they assemble? When did they form? Why did they exist? How were members added to the ranks?

Da Mongoloids began in 1994, the vision of seventeen-years-old Junior Sanchez and Armand Van Helden, who were joined by Sneak to form its core. Mutual love and respect of Chicago House genera connecting them. An entity of forward-thinking producers focused on the growth of electronic music and its culture, unafraid to bridge the gap between the underground and pop, the dancefloor as its primary meter.

Armand Van Helden explained the genesis of the crew in our fall 1996 interview.

"A lot of people are in it, but it's not like we've gotten it all together yet. It's almost like we're tryin' to create a Wu-Tang of House. That's what the Mongoloids is. I got a younger crew already called Da Mongoloids. It's these younger heads, these fourteen, fifteen-year-old heads. They're coming up, and they wanna be down. They'll be over at my house, we'll be crackin' beats, and they're 'Yo! How can I be down with that Mongoloids shit." And it be, 'Yo! You can be down with the Mongoloids. Get your own clique,' and they go alright. Boom! It's some crazy shit. It don't even make sense but we throwin' it together and seein' what happens. I can tell you that DJ Sneak, Frankie Feliciano, Junior Sanchez, a lot of the Constipated Monkey's people from Kurious's crew. I don't know if you know much about Hip-Hop, people from Artifacts. There's different people connected in with it, but it's House. We've rolled before. We've rolled up in clubs, and people go 'Oh look, it's the Mongoloids,' and shit, whatever. So, we said alright, we're gonna keep that shakin'. It's for fun. It's some bugged shit."

Da Mongoloids manifested into a music entity in September 1996, when Strictly Rhythm issued the single official 12" produced and mixed by Armand Van Helden, "Spark Da Meth." "It's Chicago House meets Hip-Hop and a touch of Daft Punk," proclaimed Van Helden in May 1997. Junior Sanchez's bold graffiti Mongoloids lettering was adorning its cover. Its label shouting-out the next generation.

Bear Who?, Erick Morillo, Kaiser Soze, Junior Sanches
Armand Van Helden, Roger Sanchez, Harry Romero, DJ Sneak, Gavin Gerbz

"Sho-Outs for Da Fno-Ons: Sneak, Cajmere, Gu, Paul Johnson, Joe Lewis, Traxhead Steve, Boo Williams, Gene Farris, Johnny Fiasco, and Da Rest of the Relief Mafia. Thomas Bangalter, Dave Clarke, Dog Trax, Robert Armani, Joey Beltram, Pierre, Jamez & Dobre. X-Mix. Davey Dee. Johnny D. Common Sense & Method Man for Da Stylos. Step into the cypher, Son. -Mongoloids coming for ya castle in da nine-6."

In an unreleased 2015 interview with Armand Van Helden and Junior Sanchez at Ibiza's Cafe Mambo, Steve Aoki asked Da Mongoloids founders to speak on the crew's connection to Daft Punk, and Van Helden replied: "Daft Punk's early career, their first releases, were also entirely ripping Cajmere's Relief Records label. When we heard these guys, we didn't know them from a hole in the wall. We played it, and we're like, 'This sounds like Relief Records but mixed way better, right?' It was like the mix downs; these things were jumping, the mixing was super. The Relief Records were more like ghetto tracks, you know. These were bouncing off the record. We were like who are these guys? One year we went down to Miami, we went to the music conference, and Junior said 'Yo, I think that's Daft Punk.' I was like 'What? Really?' When somebody goes to you 'Do you want to meet Daft Punk,' in 1995, you weren't like freaking out, you were like yeah, cool. It was cool; I'll meet Daft Punk, sure. But, it wasn't like you're gonna drool. It got to a point where Thomas, Pedro, Guy, everybody was just like 'Hey, we should do a record.'

Erick Morillo pumps it up as Armand Van Helden and DJ Sneak marvel at his stength.

Roger Sanchez

The Rhythm, the Traxx, the Basement Jaxx

Bear Who?

I was like 'Hell no!' I kinda almost like it that's it's a mystery. I almost don't want it to be a real thing. First of all, there's too many chefs in the kitchen. I remember, everybody looked at me like 'Damn, Armand's not down with doing it,' and dude, I totally regret."

Thomas Bangalter first crossed paths with Da Mongoloids when he handed DJ Sneak a copy of ***Trax On Da Rocks*** at a Paris party. Armand Van Helden was the first person to remix a Daft Punk song with his "*Ten Minutes of Funk*" Mix of "Da Funk." Roger Sanchez and Junior Sanchez were invited to remix "*Revolution 909.*" Daft Punk remixing "*Chord Memory*" for Ian Pooley, and Pooley returning the favour by remixing "*Burnin.*" Sneak also remixing "*Burnin*," and alongside Roger Sanchez and Junior Sanchez marked a cameo in its filmed in Chicago video. Sneak further collaborating with Guy-Manuel de Homem-Christo and Rico The Wizard.

Da Mongoloids brotherhood "consisting of some heads" proliferating to a League of Extraordinary Gentlemen leading the next generation of House music.

Mongoloids lore was omnipresent in the core dance music community.

A brotherhood advancing the music, crashing the charts, selling out international clubs, demanding and getting astronomical remix fees, and changing the game. A wellspring of musical inspiration connecting them. Interest in Da Mongoloids was percolating ensuing the 1997 Miami Winter Music Conference. *The Mongoloids Tour* stopping at Toronto's Industry Nightclub, Sunday, May 18, 1997. A Victoria Day long-weekend, in honour of Queen Victoria, who reigned over the United Kingdom of Great Britain and Ireland from 1837-1901.

Roger S, Armand Van Helden, Erick Morillo, DJ Sneak, and Harry Romero.

The notorious Mongoloids throwing down one night only: Armand Van Helden, DJ Sneak, Junior Sanchez, and Erick "More" Morillo. With a Unabomber live P.A. courtesy of Mario J and Vince Ailey. Roger Sanchez, Bear Who? (Mongoloids tattooed on his arm), Harry Romero, and Kaiser Soze representing in the City. (Daft Punk, Ian Pooley, Basement Jaxx, Rhythm Masters and Jacques Lu Cont (Stuart Price) filling out the collective at the time).

A real Wu-Tang Clan mentality towards House music. A lineup of the ages, and a press conference in order. The legendary crew sat as one, responding to questions by a handful of independent media, and made themselves available for one-on-one interviews.

"If Wu-Tang did it, we could do it with House. We could do something positive towards House," said DJ Sneak.

Roger S. breaks it down as Erick Morillo contemplates spending "I Like To Move It" loot.

Erick "More" Morillo wants to know Are You ready For Some More?

"The difference with us is no one person is bigger or more important than the other," added elder statesman, Roger Sanchez. "Each one of us has our individual strengths and rather than coming together and having one figurehead for it, which almost naturally you would have thought would be Armand or myself, or Erick, or Sneak. It's more like we all come together and form a collective head. In other words, that we all say alright, this is how we're going to approach this."

The dualities of dance music and its stigma that were branded Electronica at the time, succinctly captured by the smooth-spoken Roger Sanchez.

"It's funny, because it's almost like saying Kraftwerk it's a brand new band, and they're electronica. They were pioneers. Dance music has been around. Part of the problem is it's got astigmatism in

America. It's got the gay stigmatism, Black minority stigmatism, and major white America doesn't want to know about it. Electronica probably has a drug stigmatism, not probably, it has a drug stigmatism too. I don't think that's the big concern. The big concern is it's quote-unquote the next big thing. What people have to realise is that the talent has been there for a long time. We've been doing this for years, and the thing is that one of the outcomes of the changing environment and climate in terms of consumers in America for music has resulted in people like us getting together and saying 'Right, we've been doing this shit for years, building up our individual strengths. Let's get together and let's change this. I may not like the term electronica. I'm glad people are finally paying attention to what we're doing. To me, and to most of us, it's a big laugh saying 'See, we knew what we did could sell. People were too stupid to see it until somebody put a label on it.'

Armand Van Helden and Strictly Rhythm A&R prophet, Gladys Pizarro @ WMC 1997.

But at the same time, people are now getting into it, which is good."

By spring 1998, Da Mongoloids axiom had reached a fever pitch, embracing a special handshake and tribal 'Ayak' greeting.

"Da Mongoloids is ridiculously growing. It's a little bit out of my hands," related Armand Van Helden in our spring 1998 interview. "I'm down with everybody and everything; it's all love within the whole thing. But when you crew up with a lot of different people, everybody's on a different head. It's all love if anything it means that we can all hang out and there's no animosity, which is nice, and everybody clicks. It's giving respect for each other within the whole Mongoloid camp.

Colonel Matt C, Cajmere, Armand Van Helden, and DJ Sneak in the ugliest shirt ever.

"Rhythm Masters are down now. We met them in Miami, and Junior is like 'Yo! Let's make them Mongoloids.' So whatever, they're Mongoloids. It's like if we respect and like somebody's music chances are they're gonna be a Mongoloid (laughs).In terms of the organisation of it all, it's all over the place. It's not organised. It's not like it exists. It's something that's there, and I like it that way. It's like, if you know about it you know about it. If you don't, we ain't pushing it on you. It's something that means we can click, like Basement Jaxx coming to New York, they give me a call, they're Mongoloids. They're like Daft Punk, Sneak, Roger S., Erick, whatever. It means that we can hang out and we're not throwing drama at everybody because in the Hip-Hop and House world, all the worlds in music you got a lot of competition between camps and these types of things. To me, it's old. The only thing about Da Mongoloids is usually it's newer people 'cause I can't grab from the old school because they don't care. I don't know; I could be wrong. I know Kenny (Dope), and I know Louie (Vega), and I know Todd (Terry) and all of them, but I don't think they care. They know Da Mongoloids. They go 'What's up with this Mongoloids shit?' But they're - I think it's a new wave thing.' It's mostly new jacks, and we come together on a new jack type basis."

Unfortunately, this period of high-calibre Mongoloids bred success led a few astray, complacent, and with it, individual members of the brotherhood began branding single releases and remixes as Mongoloid.

"Me, I started the thing, and I'm the least one involved with all of it," responded Van Helden in our spring 1998 interview. "It's funny because everybody else took it to the level, I didn't. The original setup with me and Junior. Then it was Junior, Sneak, and me. After that, that's when we started to camp everybody in; it worked out fine. I don't care; I got love for everybody. I'm distant with it. I love it for what it is. In actual explanation of what we all are, no, there ain't nothin'. It means that we can hang, at least for me. Now I noticed some problems, everybody within it, certain problems, that's a part of life. Wu-Tang got the same shit. Anybody when you crew up in large numbers you get one or two people that get into some scenario, that's a part of life. But, the love is still there regardless, ups and down wise, the love is still there."

Inside the Times Square home studio of Armand Van Helden, 1998.

Thankfully, love maintained, for the most part. In January 2000, Da Mongoloids core consisting of Armand Van Helden, Junior Sanchez, DJ Sneak, Rpger Sanchez, Ian Pooley, and Basement Jaxx. Other members were continuing to drift in and out of the ranks. Armand Van Helden was providing another update on the crew in our January 2000 interview.

"The Mongoloids still exist, its an entity. It's camaraderie. It's a group unto itself. As long as we're friends, it's never gonna go away. We don't necessarily have to put out music together to make it last. It has nothing to do with that. It's a gang, and it's no different than when you're in the Mob. you're always in the Mob.

Even if you disappear, go off and do your thing, it's still a part of you, and that's what you believe. I'm not speaking out of my ass, but I believe that's what it is. It's something that whether we do something with it business wise or not, it's gonna be around as long as the friendships are good."

Egos and lifestyle choices notwithstanding.

"Well, that's the thing," continued Van Helden. "Most of the people in the Mongoloids, there's only a couple of strong egos. We're more intellects than we are egos. Everybody has their opinion, and everybody will usually be individuals.

S-Men in the mix on the craziest boat cruise, ever @ WMC 1997.

There's nothing wrong with that, but the ego side - some people like to glam it more than others do. We never hold that against anybody. Man, if it's there to declare, glam it; take it."

Ian Pooley was asked about the pressure of performing as a member of the heavyweight producer crew, by Steve Yanko in our fall 2000 interview promoting his *Since Then* album. The German Tech-House producer and DJ kept it pretty basic.

"No. I don't need that. People are telling me that this album is going crazy, selling so much, but I don't pay attention. Armand had this idea about three or four years ago and said immediately that I was involved. It's a respect for each other personally and production wise. I don't mind when he says I'm there because I like all the producers that are a part of it."

Guy-Manuel de Homem-Christo is summarising the brotherhood in our January 2001 interview.

Guy-Manuel de Homem-Christo surrounded by love @ WMC 2000. Who do you spot?

"We don't have any decisions about Mongoloids; I wish I had some news. We saw Roger Sanchez the other day, and Armand. Everybody is working on their stuff. That's pretty good for everybody to be pushing their music. Maybe when everybody is finished with their work, then we'll have a project. For the moment, I don't think there are much plans. We're okay with Da Mongoloids. There's no problem because everybody's been around the world. Maybe they're making an album behind my back; I don't know (laughs). I think it's just everybody's too much around the world and just meeting sometimes (laughs)."

Part Two: Discovery

(New York, New York)

Following the global success of *Homework*, it's hard to imagine how Daft Punk might follow up. The debut album sold over one million copies generating a Gold plaque in the United States, achieving Platinum status in the UK, New Zealand, and France, and double-platinum up here in Canada. Its four singles - *"Da Funk"*, *"Around the World"*, *"Burnin'"*, *"Revolution 909"* - driving French House to global dance music clubs and beyond.

Thomas Bangalter and Guy-Manuel de Homem-Christo toured the world until the end of 1997, releasing *"Revolution 909"* in February 1998, and disappeared from the limelight. *D.A.F.T.: A Story About Dogs, Androids, Firemen and Tomatoes*, featuring the four *Homework* singles, behind the scenes of *"Fresh"* and *"Rollin' & Scratchin'"* live in L.A. releasing November 15, 1999.

Music sounds better with you, Guy-Man.

Bangalter and de Homem-Christo continuing to work in the underground, issuing solo 12"'s and remixing others. Momentarily resurfacing at the 1999 and 2000 *Winter Music Conference*.

In Fall 2000, word of a new Daft Punk album began to filter out of Paris, France. One tale is centring on a bizarre studio accident transforming the duo into robots. In reality, Bangalter and de Homem-Christo were spending time in their home Daft House studio investigating new drum machines, synthesisers, samplers, a vocoder and an early version of Logic, putting together *Discovery*.

The first impression of *Discovery* dropped November 13, 2000. "*One More Time,*" the vocoder drove single featuring Romananthony opening and setting off the album that was created in the early stages of production back in 1998 and put on ice. The biggest selling Daft Punk record until the modern Disco classic "*Get Lucky*" in 2013. A virtual launch into commercial stardom for Romanthony that continues to turn dance-floors to this day. The early stages of *Discovery's* production were also generating "*Too Close,*" featuring Romanthony, the forerunner to the electro-R&B sounds of now. Deep thinkers and students of the game, Bangalter and de Homem-Christo then took a step back to explore unconventional song structures. Integrating vintage equipment, drawing inspiration from New York Garage, Jazz, Funk, New Wave, Minimal Techno, Baroque Orchestral Pop, and Dance Pop, to forge a masterful blend of cinematic bliss.

In January 2001; Virgin Records brought Daft Punk to New York City and invited influential media to speak with the duo in advance of the release of *Discovery*. Photographer Steven Carty, Virgin Records Canada PR, and I flew from YYZ to LGA for the cover story feature. We checked-in to our hotel, ate lunch, and jumped in a taxi to the mid-town Manhattan studio loft where we were greeted by Thomas Bangalter, Guy-Manuel de Homem-Christo, and Pedro Winter. Members of Virgin's international media were also present with a videographer to capture the session. Our vigilant mystery writer is arriving and exchanging warm greetings in French. Carty was setting up his photography equipment as we moved to sit and record Daft Punk.

With the release of *Discovery*, the most anticipated album in the history of House music, Daft Punk set no limits on success. A humble and down to earth, Thomas Bangalter disagreed.

"Well, I don't think it is the most anticipated because I remember waiting for Dave Clarke's album. Maybe it's because people are tired of waiting. I don't necessarily think that it is the most anticipated. I think when we did *Homework* people didn't know what to expect and we were not using the proper marketing and promotional channels. The music spoke for itself."

Whereas the rhythmical driving forces of Techno and House defined *Homework*, *Discovery* existed to open up the dance music community to a wide range of music in its indomitable endeavour to break down barriers and staid categories. Its broad range of musical evolution leading purists to claim Daft Punk had ceased to exist. Thomas Bangalter broke down the logical progression and thought process behind broadening the scope of music.

Bow-wow-wow-yippie-yo-yippie-yeah

"Everybody's free to do what they want. We like the idea of having maybe one sound, but not having one style precisely. We record and do music the same way we used to, but we'd like to have an open mind. We like the idea Electronic and House music as being about destroying the old rules and to set up new rules at the same time. We want to destroy the new rules as well. The labels and the categories were something that was set up by the system and by the media and the record labels to sell the music. 'Okay, so what are you? Are you Heavy Metal? Are you Soul? Are you Disco?' House was pretty much about destroying those barriers, but then now that it's accepted in a way, it's like are you Heavy Metal, or are you House music? If you're House music, then you have to do ten-minute soundtracks with one idea or two. It's interesting, but House music to us is more about the spirit that should be breaking those categories."

Homework delivered a new realm to the world of electronic music in 1997. Accessible to the point it crossed over to the mainstream selling over one million copies. Core to the end it filled dancefloors. Thomas Bangalter's Stardust project dominating the summer of 1998, with the anthemic "*Music Sounds Better With You*." The anticipated November 13, 2000 release of "One More Time" igniting the international scene declaring Daft Punk season in effect, again.

Naturally, the underground dance music community feared to lose the group to commercial success. Thomas Bangalter shook his head at the notion.

"We don't know what the word 'commercial' means. We're not preventing Daft Punk from becoming popular if people like it, or becoming unpopular because people don't like it.

We're just doing things that we were still doing, and anyway, the word 'underground' in Europe doesn't mean anything anymore. The music that used to be underground is popular now and sells lots of records. So it's selling a lot of records and becoming commercial. If being commercial meant making music to please the people and not please yourself then it would be different, but that's not the way we do it. I think a lot of people didn't know what to expect from *Homework* and they might not know what to expect from *Discovery* because *Discovery* is very different from *Homework*. Being commercial might be just what we've been doing with *Homework* and everything else."

Are We Not Men? We Are Daft Punk!

In sync with the musical evolution and revolution of Daft Punk, Hip-Hop and R&B producers began to integrate the pulse of House and Techno tempting a full diverse demographic with dancefloor appeal reaching new commercial heights. Mannie Fresh was connecting the southern Gangsta Rap of Cash Money Records New Orleans call and response Bounce to Miami Bass utilising samples and 808 loops. Timbaland, Swizz Beatz, and The Neptunes building number one hits on synth riffs and keyboards.

Indeed, Daft Punk lay years ahead of the curve. The electro-funk and soul of *Discovery* an aural roadmap to the sounds of today, living to inspire purveyors of post-Disco French House and auto-tune architects.

My Kingdom for a pair of clean sneakers.

An omen of future studio sessions and collaborations with Kanye West, Pharrell Williams, Nile Rodgers, and The Weeknd. The duo spoke on the influence of Hip-Hop producers and possible collaboration. Maybe you got more House producers that are digging Hip-Hop and do some downtempo tracks than you have Hip-Hop producers that make House beats," said Guy-Manuel de Homem-Christo. "But, at this moment it's very exciting. OutKast, Neptunes, and Rockwilder especially, who has the electronic sound. In House music, people tend to try different things, but we're still not making music together. So, the next step is for us to make music with them, or for them to make music for us. Not us, but just House producers. Maybe it already exists, just not on a larger scale."

"No collaborations, but, trying different tempos and styles," added Thomas Bangalter. "I think we've done it. And there are different influences on *Discovery* and already on *Homework*. The issue is not about Hip-Hop, House, Heavy Metal, Soul, Funk, Country, Punk or whatever. At the end of the day, it's just music. The most interesting things that have happened with producers in Hip-Hop or House are not House producers who want to get closer to Hip-Hop or Hip-Hop producers who want to get closer to House, but more producers that can take influences

I wish The Wizard was on this trip.

from any style of music and that are open-minded and are trying to break the barriers. The labels themselves in Hip-Hop, in House, are defined by what has been done and not what's going to be done. In the beginning, it was done without samples and synthesisers and drum machines, and then after there were samples, and synthesisers and drum machines, and then after there were samples, so people began to define House as this and that. Maybe it won't mean anything anymore, like Rock from the 60s and then Pop Rock in the 80s to the 90s, and it kept getting bigger and bigger until it didn't mean anything anymore. But it's in a good way because it's only music that touches people. The music stays pretty much the same. It might be done in home studios or bigger studios, but the instruments themselves, from us to Eminem, to Britney Spears, are pretty much the same."

Fast forward to 2007. Kanye West inserted a vocoder sample of "*Harder, Faster, Better, Faster*" on "*Stronger.*" West and his team allegedly mixing it over seventy-five times, working with eight audio engineers, and eleven mix engineers. Finally retaining Timbaland to revitalise its drum programming before approving it for his *Graduation* album. West unhappy to the bitter end claiming it failed to live up to the Daft Punk original. "*Stronger*" hit number one on the charts in Canada, New Zealand, Turkey, UK, and the U.S., selling over seven million copies in the U.S., and winning the Grammy Award for **Best Rap Solo Performance** at the 50th Annual Grammy Awards. The song inspiring Hip-Hop producers to blend House and Electro in their

Toute l'année nous prépare une journée de reve.

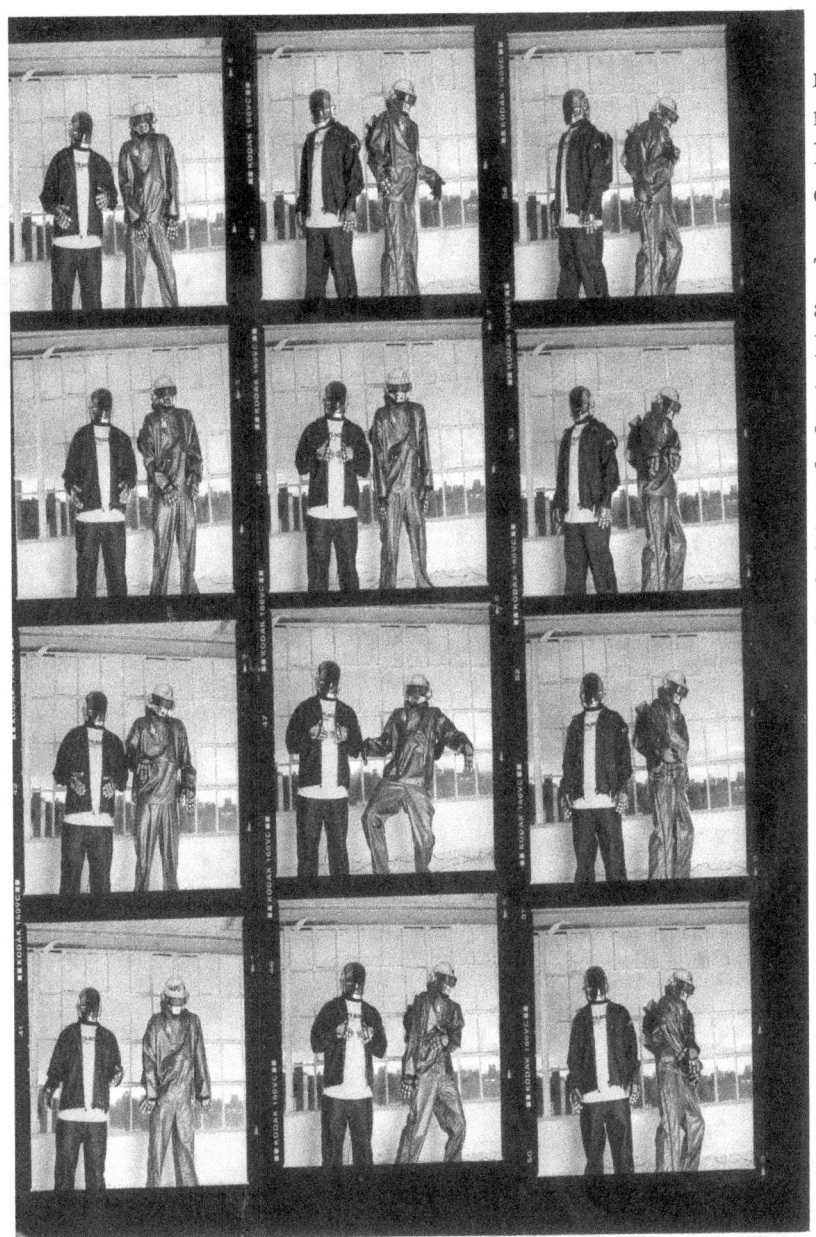

Contact sheet by Steve Carty

music, and playing a part in the resurgence of the Art Forms and Daft Punk's rise in mainstream culture.

The relationship between Hip-Hop and R&B coming full circle with Daf Punk co-producing four songs - "*I Am God,*" "*Send It Up,*" "*On Sight,*" "*Black Skinhead*" - on West's critically acclaimed 2013 album, *Yeezus*. Bangalter and de Homem-Christo going on to co-produce and feature on two singles - "*Starboy,*" and "*I Feel It Coming*" - off The Weeknd's *Starboy* album generating over one billion streams in 2017.

The unyielding desire of Daft Punk to innovate while refusing to be tied to any direct or indirect movement attempting to penetrate its music and image, whatsoever. Illustrated within the heart of all output, from songs and remixes to graphics and videos, soundtracks and films.

Bangalter and de Homem-Christo the break the rules guys when it came to codified standards of engagement.

"Innovating means breaking the rules and broaden music and not buying into the system," explained Bangalter. "It's never been like, 'Okay, someone is doing it like that. We want to be like him.' It's more like, 'Okay, someone is doing something different. We'd also like to do something different.' So there must be other people like us in the world."

"We have to learn from the outside about doing something new," added de Homem-Christo. "Maybe just by naturally wanting to do something else. Maybe some people are always doing the same thing, especially in this House or Disco style of music. It's too boring to do the same thing again and again.

Contact sheet by Steve Carty

Contact sheet by Steve Carty

House music right now is not just about Chicago, or Disco House, or Funk and Disco samples. (But) Radiohead, OutKast, Bjork; people that aren't trapped in their categories and that are not allowing people to label them."

"Maybe this has to do with the fact that in House music people felt free to do anything because it was underground and there was a lot of freedom," concluded Bangalter. The fact that it started to be popular or having more impact these people that are making the music are under more pressure. They cannot have the same freedom that they used to have, and it's not true. They should try to take risks and do certain things to surprise themselves and surprise the people."

Nor shall this peace sleep with her; but as when
The bird of wonder dies, the maiden phoenix,
Her ashes new create another heir
As great in admiration as herself;
So shall she leave her blessedness to one,
When heaven shall call her from this cloud of darkness,
Who from the sacred ashes of her honour
Shall star-like rise as great in fame as she was,
And so stand fix'd.

William Shakespeare, Henry VIII

Green Velvet, AKA Cajmere, has blurred the lines between House and Techno as the man behind the Cajual and Relief labels. A Chemical Engineer by trade, he may not be on the nuclear edge like Homer Simpson, but he is in his world. A player since '92, when he unleashed the classic "Percolator," other hot records to his credit include "The Preacher Man," "Brighter Days," and "Answering Machine." The release of his Electro-Funk meets Jack House *Constant Chaos* album a few months away, he spoke with Andy Roberts in summer 1998, of a new school of thought within the international dance music community affecting both the music and clubs.

"People wanted things to go in a more pop feel or direction. Whereas, I only see stuff as underground. Even though the Green Velvet stuff is getting more successful, I view it as an underground format. I don't think the goal is to sell thousands and thousands of records. That shouldn't be the main objective in underground music because what's the point of being underground. The way the people view success in it is a little messed up sometimes because some tracks may become big sellers. That's not the way the scene should go, and it's not like anybody who is not doing that should be looked at like this is bad, 'You only sold 500 records! Your shit sucks!' It should not be viewed as that because you can't have cutting-edge music if everything has an expectation put on it. What happened with the industry messed it up 'cause you get a lot of who started trying to monopolise on what happened. The people who were throwing the cool underground parties couldn't stay in it that much; I'm talking about a worldwide thing. You start getting people throwing these huge parties, and then all of a sudden, people as far as the general public, they aren't that interested in going to a small little bar because they're like 'Well shit, I wanna go to this party where everyone's gonna be. Why am I gonna go to this little party, and blah, blah, blah.'"

Contact sheet by Steve Carty

Ignoring the sense of a mental edge when producing music is done at peril. Notably, when directed towards the heart of dance music culture divided by the spoils of success. The yin and yang of measuring and weighing the prizes of underground and mainstream adulation against the need and desire to further the Art Form. To move the music forward until its soaring overhead, a metaphorical Phoenix rising from the ashes.

"The people want to keep things confidential, but then it's not underground anymore," pointed out de Homem-Christo. "Take Europe, for example. In Europe, the underground scene has become overground, and as Thomas often says, there's no difference between underground and overground. The only difference is the network. The music is the same.

"Maybe in the U.S., it's better to stay underground, but once you get rich, you cannot stay in a home studio. You make a record that gets big, that makes it, and you get signed by a major company, maybe before it was on an independent label. But as soon as it gets the recognition, it becomes mainstream music. Maybe you still have some people that like the underground to exist and keep everything confidential. Rock, it's not underground anymore. It doesn't matter if it's underground or commercial, it's a fact that underground means confidential and it's not confidential anymore."

"Which is what we've been fighting for, and I think a lot of people have been fighting for, but at the same time, once the battle is won people start to regret the old times of being a minority," expounded Bangalter.

Contact sheet by Steve Carty

"It's true for a lot of people there's no point in trying to demonstrate that over and over. It becomes redundant like a veteran's speech. 'Yes! Let's make this music accepted.' Now all the governments, all those systems, those institutions, they've pretty much accepted this music, and now it's this big corporate thing. Now, the only thing that matters after this is the music. It will be the same way for people that believe in this music to sell records, but that exists in both the independent channels and the corporate channels. You've got people at independent labels, and even though it's independent, it's cool that they're making music for the fun of it, and then you have other people making music to make money. You have artists at major labels who try to make the best music and at the same time make money, but it used to be much more simple and much more precise. Where the underground was the cool thing and the corporate was evil, and now there's as much innovation, as much evil, as much cool thing or not, and good music and commercial music are on both networks. That's where everybody is freaking out at some points. Teenager you wants to be part of something. You want to belong to a subculture, and you want to fight for it to be accepted. Once the subculture gets accepted, it's a great thing because you were a part of it, but then you're not part of subculture anymore. Maybe you can realise that it's good to be open-minded because it's not subculture because it has to be. It's subculture because it's worth being in it if this is accepted. But other people it's good, and maybe it's good to be a part of that. The other thing is once it's accepted, you should rest for a time, which is okay, rather than keep trying on. For us, as musicians or producers is to know that the next step is by innovating and experimenting again. The differences are maybe experimenting now. You're not scared of keeping it completely underground. This is very new because there hasn't been that much freedom in the past to experiment widely. *Discovery*, even if it's not accepted, we feel good for not being in the same state we were five years ago. Some people sometimes regret that. That wouldn't be House music, to focus on the past. House is pretty much something that has to move to the present. We were not part of the Summer of Love in '88, but this happens only once, and it's a great thing for people to have been a part of that. You are not going to try to do Summer of Love '98."

Contact sheet by Steve Carty

This is the question of Daft Punk and *Discovery*. The exceptional line thoroughbred creatives straddle yet fear to cross. Breed success, take the money and run. Risk being branded a sellout and end up locked out of the core structure you helped build. Though, in the case of Daft Punk, it can hardly be termed a dilemma when the combatants refuse to care about the outcome. The danger and perception more significant than the reality.

"You have two kinds of people that are into House music," interpreted Bangalter. "You have people that are into changing things globally, so it can be to make this music widely accepted. Then you have other people that want to keep it underground and confidential because if it's confidential people feel more like they're part of a secret society. Either you're organising the revolution; then once the revolution is global, you're selling out.

By selling out you're doing it not for the principal, you're doing it to make money. The other is if you want to be part of a secret society, then you're very angry at people. For us, we want music shared. Maybe some people want to keep the music for five friends and knowing the new hot stuff. We think differently. Something really good for everybody, to show it to more people it's a good feeling. It's music, and it's supposed to be bringing people together."

Steve Carty preparing for the photo shoot.

Discovery promotional folder.

Let it be understood; Daft Punk was not the lone purveyors of French House and Techno. An interchangeable force percolated amongst a crucial few fellow citizens responsible for furthering the music on their terms.

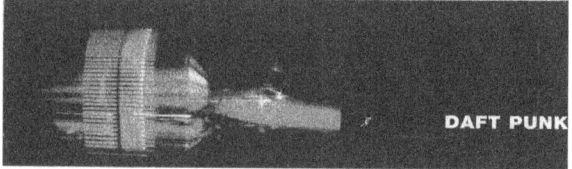

Pioneering DJ and composer, Laurent Garnier began to play House and Techno in 1987 and remains an international force to this day.

Superstar DJ, David Guetta played Hip-Hop and House in clubs at the age of seventeen, "French Touch" parties in 1987, and also led the French takeover of Ibiza.

Speaking of the rich influence of Motorbass and Daft Punk in our 2009 interview, he said, "Honestly, I didn't take anything. First, these are my friends, and they've opened doors for us in a huge way.

Thomas Bangalter even helped me connect with Virgin Records after I made "*Love Is Gone.*" But the Daft Punk guys changed dance music history – and, I think, music history period. At that time it was so big and came with a sound that was so totally different - but I can't say I followed them because my sound was more electro."

Ludovic Navarre, AKA St Germain, was instrumental in developing the French Touch with the *Motherland EP* and *French Traxx EP* in 1993. His sophisticated and elegant *Tourist* album of 2000, eschewing filtered loops for Jazz and Deep House, sold over three million copies worldwide. Though in our summer 2000 interview with Andy Roberts, when asked from where he drew his influence for the album, he said, "As usual; Blues, Soul, Funk, and Jazz from the sixties and seventies. I hardly listen to anything contemporary, and I certainly don't listen to the 'French Touch' scene. I am also very interested in World Music."

Chicago House and sparkling undertones of deep Detroit Techno is palpable in the music of Motorbass. Its members Phillippe Zdar, who went on to become one-half of Cassius alongside Boom Bass, and Etienne de Crécy of *Super Discount* fame, both together and individually principal players. "With Motorbass, the good thing was we were independent, and we were totaliser. We didn't ask to do something," said Zdar to Andy Roberts in our 1999 interview.

To a loose extent, Dimitri from Paris, and Air. Nicolas Godin and Jean-Benoit Dunckel of Air beginning their career recording simplistic downtempo instrumental tracks like "*Modular*" and "*Cassanova 70,*" to radio-friendly pop with hooks and vocals using vintage analogue instruments. Etienne de Crécy placing the repetitive themes, melodies and samples of their improvised playing into his effects-laden mixing board. Sounds of the progressive French dancefloor influencing Godin and Dunckel evident in the melancholic flow of "*Le Soleil est Pres de Moi.*"

"We love club music in Paris, and we are very humbled by that music because it is something we are unable to do," emphasised Godin in our January 1998 interview with Nav Sangha. "For example, if you take Daft Punk. I often go to their studio, and we have the same sort of equipment; samplers, old keyboards, vocoders, but we do such different things with it. It's incredible because if we had the choice, we would probably make dance music more like that, but we are unable to do that. It's not in us. If we don't put drums in a song, it's because we have no idea of how to do those rhythms. It's not a choice for us - it happens that way. This is why our songs are remixed by people like La Funk Mob and Motorbass because we like clubbing, but the problem is that when we make music, it is sometimes better for sleeping than clubbing. The remixes of "*Sexy Boy*" turned out very interesting. La Funk Mob have found an open door for what can come after House. For the first time, I preferred the remix to the original - when I heard it, I said, wow, the song should be exactly like that."

Air was enjoying the hype surrounding producers from the French scene. However, they did so with a sense of apprehension. "The great moments for pop music in France were in the 50s and 60s with great singers such as Jacques Brel and Serge Gainsborough," proclaimed Dunckel. "But then in the 70s and 80s, the world noticed nothing. At this moment, the new fashionable style is French again, but in one year it could be Spanish or something else."

Substantially, the music of French artists grew legs infiltrating its way out of European dance music strongholds through Ibiza and as far as Canada. The scarcity of Daft Punk in the four-years between *Homework* and *Discovery* compelling enthusiastic fans to explore other French artists. French House, often cited as the "French Touch", becoming a thing. Thomas Bangalter was responsible for guiding Modjo to sample Chic's "*Soup For One*" on their tremendous single, "*Lady (Hear Me Tonight).*"

"The French Touch, when you look at singles, naturally there has been some disco loops; therefore it was easier for the media to make that assumption, but when you look closely at the albums that came out of France, they were very different from one to another," propagated Bangalter. "We're on a French label; some artists are not. When you look at the albums and the artists they're all pretty much different. Music is something for people to have fun and to dance, and to feel in a very spontaneous way. Naturally, we are interested in trying to break the rules and do new things, but that's not the unique thing about our music. Music can be about picking a non-traditional formula and doing it good and doing it well, and transmitting something on emotion or something that people feel. Modjo is a good example of that. Maybe they're not reinventing music with what they're doing, but good at what they do. A lot of people are touched, and that's a good thing. It's different music. Everybody's free to do what they want."

"Oh, what's the matter with the crowd I'm seeing?
"Don't you know that they're out of touch?"
Well, should I try to be a straight-A student?
"If you are then you think too much. Don't you know about the new fashion, honey?
All you need are looks and a whole lotta money."
It's the next phase, new wave, dance craze, anyways
It's still rock and roll to me
Everybody's talkin' 'bout the new sound
Funny, but it's still rock and roll to me.

Billy Joel "It's Still Rock N' Roll To Me" (1980)

The dance music club scene is notorious for its wild atmosphere, and the vice of DJs entrenched in the five-star life. The after-party surely the stuff of legend. Our time coming to an end I ask one more question..

Where do the groupies fit in?

"It's very embarrassing, I don't know what it is, but I see all these girls on tour, so many girls all the time," responded Guy-Manuel de Homem-Christo. "We've never been in the situation of being like N'Sync or Backstreet Boys. They are the Pop stars of the time. I don't even know how they do it because after the show you're tired. We try to have fun and would rather just be chilling. We're not different from you or anybody. We've never been in the situation of having groupies around because it's not what we want, and it's not our way of living. That's not why we like music."

Thomas Bangalter smiled and polished off the interview.

"That's a very serious answer for a very funny question. The world is full of discovery and secrets. A lot of things that we can see, but it's not just about groupies. People tend to consider the grass is always greener on the other side."

Straight talk by Thomas Bangalter and Guy-Manuel de Homem-Christo. Everybody is free to be you and me. It's a lovely sentiment and critical insight into the mindset that turned the fortune of dance music.

What's in a name? What is House music? What is Techno music? Heavy Metal? There is only good music and bad music. Either it moves you, or it doesn't.

Discovery was released February 26, 2001. It generated Gold plaques in Australia, Belgium, Canada, Germany, Switzerland, and the United States. Platinum plaques in Denmark and Japan, Double-Platinum in the UK, and Triple-Platinum in France. Its six singles - *"One More Time", "Aerodynamic", "Digital Love", "Harder, Better, Faster, Stronger", "Face to Face",* and *"Something About Us"* spanning from November 2000 to November 2003. It is approaching worldwide sales of three million copies.

DISCOGRAPHY

ALBUMS

STUDIO

Homework – January 17, 1997 (Virgin/Soma)

Discovery – February 26, 2001 (Virgin)

Human After All – March 14, 2005 (Virgin)

Random Access Memories – May 17, 2013 (Columbia)

LIVE

Alive 1997 – October 1, 2001 (Virgin) recorded November 8, 1997 @ Qué Club, Birmingham

Alive 2007 – November 19, 2007 (Virgin) recorded June 14, 2007 @ Bercy (Paris, France).

VIDEO COLLECTION

D.A.F.T.: A Story About Dogs, Androids, Firemen and Tomatoes – November 1, 2000 (Virgin)

DAFT PUNK
"Human After All"

1.	HUMAN AFTER ALL	5:20
2.	THE PRIME TIME OF YOUR LIFE	4:23
3.	ROBOT ROCK	4:26
4.	STEAM MACHINE	5:21
5.	MAKE LOVE	4:49
6.	THE BRAINWASHER	4:08
7.	ON/OFF	0:19
8.	TELEVISION RULES THE NATION	4:46
9.	TECHNOLOGIC	4:43
10.	EMOTION	6:57

121 Harris Rosen Peace

Virgin records

PLEASE SEE REVERSE FOR CONDITIONS OF USE.

COMPILATION ALBUM

Musique Vol. 1 1993-2005 – March 29, 2006 (Virgin)

SOUNDTRACK

Interstella 5555: The 5tory of the 5ecret 5tar 5ystem –May 18, 2003 (Virgin) directed by Kazuhisa Takenouchi

Electroma – May 21, 2006 (Daft Arts/Wild Bunch) directed by Daft Punk

Tron: Legacy – December 3, 2010 (Walt Disney Records)

REMIX ALBUM

Daft Club – December 2, 2003 (Virgin)

Human After All: Remixes – March 29, 2006 (Toshiba/EMI) Japan

Tron: Legacy Reconfigured – April 5, 20011 (Walt Disney Records)

SINGLES

"The New Wave"/"Assault"/"Alive" EP - April 11, 1994 (Soma Quality Recordings)

"Da Funk" - 1995 (Soma Quality Recordings)

"Indo Silver Club" - February 26, 1996 (Soma Quality Recordings)

"Around The World" - March 17, 1997 (Virgin)

"Burnin'" - September 22, 1997 (Virgin)

"Revolution 909" - February 16, 1998 (Virgin)

"One More Time" - November 13, 2000 (Virgin)

"Aerodynamic" - March 28, 2001 (Virgin)

"Digital Love" - June 11, 2001 (Virgin)

"Harder, Better, Faster, Stronger" (**Alive 2007**) - October 13, 2001 (Virgin)

"Face To Face" - October 10, 2003 (Virgin)

"Something About Us" - November 14, 2003 (Virgin)

"Robot Rock" - April 11, 2005 (Virgin)

"Technologic" - June 14, 2005 (Virgin)

"Human After All" - October 31, 2005 (Virgin)

"The Prime Time of Your Life" - June 17, 2006 (Virgin)

"Harder, Better, Faster, Stronger" - October 15, 2007 (Virgin)

"*Derezzed*" - December 8, 2010 (Walt Disney Records)

"*Get Lucky*" - April 19, 2013 (Columbia)

"*Lose Yourself to Dance*" - August 13, 2013 (Columbia)

"*Doin' It Right*" - September 3, 2013 (Columbia)

"*Instant Crush*" - November 22, 2013 (Columbia)

"*Give Life Back to Music*" - January 31, 2014 (Columbia)

RECORD STORE DAY

Translucence EP - April 16, 2011 (Walt Disney)
Three tracks from **Tron Legacy** and "*Castor*" previously unreleased

DARLIN'

Guy-Manuel de Homem-Christo, Thomas Bangalter, Laurent Brancowitz

Shimmies In Super 8 compilation April 1993 (Duophonic)

"*Cindy So Loud*"
"*Darlin'*"

De La Viande Pour Le Disco? 1995 (Banana Split) cassette compilation

"*Untitled (18)*"
"*Untitled (33)*"

COLLABORATION

Manu Le Malin – *Memory EP* "M18" 1995 (IST/Industrial Strength Records) produced, mixed, recorded as Draft Ponk

Two Years Together compilation "Beta Wax" with DJ Kevin 1995 (Coda) gift with Coda Magazine subscription

Teriyaki Boys - *Beef Or Chicken* - "HeartBreaker" November 16, 2005 (Def Jam Japan) produced

N.E.R.D. - *Nothing* "Hypnotize U" October 16, 2010 (Star Trak Entertainment/ Interscope Records) co-written, producer, all instruments

LCD Soundsystem – "Losing My Edge" The Long Goodbye live remix April 2, 2011 (DFA)

Kanye West – *Yeesuz*
"I Am God" May 6, 2013 (Def Jam) co-producer
"Send It Up" June 9, 2013 (Def Jam) co-producer
"On Sight" June 18, 2013 (Def Jam) producer
"Black Skinhead" June 18, 2013 (Def Jam) producer

Pharrell Williams *G I R L* "Gust Of Wind" March 3, 2014 album version, October 24, 2014 extended version (Columbia) co-written and vocal hook

Parcels - "Overnight" June 21, 2017 (Kitsuné Music/Daft Trax) co-written and co-produced

FEATURED ARTIST

The Weeknd - *Starboy*
"Starboy" September 22, 2016 (XO/Republic)
"I Feel It Coming" November 24, 2016 (XO/Republic)

REMIXES

The Micronauts – *"Get Funky Get Down"* 1995 (Micronauts)

The Chemical Brothers – *"Life Is Sweet"* August 28, 1995 (Freestyle Dust)

Gabrielle – *"Forget About the World"* April 1996 (Go! Discs)

I:Cube – *"Disco Cubism"* July 1996 (Versatile)

Ian Pooley – *"Chord Memory"* 1996 (Force Inc. Music Works)

Scott Grooves featuring Parliament & Funkadelic – *"Mothership Reconnection"* November 16, 1998 (Soma)

Franz Ferdinand - *"Take Me Out"* June 21, 2004 (Domino)

THOMAS BANGALTER

SOUNDTRACK

Original Soundtrack from the Motion Picture Irréversible – May 30, 2002 (Roulé)

First Point
Richard Phillips short starring Lindsay Lohan (June 2012)

EP

Trax on Da Rocks
"On Da Rocks" "Roulé Boulé" "What To Do" "Outrun" "Ventura" 1995 (Roulé)
Trax on Da Rocks Vol. 2
"Club Soda" "Extra Dry" Shuffle!" "Colossus" "Turbo" October 1998 (Roulé)

SINGLES

"*Spinal Scratch*" "*Spinal Beats*" 1996 (Roulé)

"*Outrage*" "*Night Beats*" "*Paris by Night*" March 6, 2003 (Roulé)

REMIXES

Alan Braxe
"*Vertigo (Virgo Edit)*" October 27, 1997 (Roulé)

Roy Davis Jr
"*Rock Shock*" (*Thomas Bangalter's Start-Stop Mix*) April 2, 1998 (Roulé)

DJ Mehdi
"*Signatune*" (*Thomas Bangalter Edit*) March 1, 2007 (Ed Banger Records)

COLLABORATION

Stardust with Alan Braxe and Benjamin Diamond
"Music Sounds Better With You" – July 20, 1998 (Roulé)

Bob Sinclair
"Gym Tonic" with James Andrew "Gym" Dakin (1998)

Phoenix
United "Embuscade" June 8, 2000 (Virgin/Source)
Synthesiser [Yamaha Cs-60]

Together with DJ Falcon
"Together" – August 2000 (Roulé)
"So Much Love to Give" – December 2002 (Roulé)

113
"113 Fout La Merde !" VS Thomas Bangalter May 7, 2002 (Small)

Arcade Fire
Everything Now album July 28, 2017
(Sonovox/Columbia) co-producer

"Everything Now" June 1, 2017 co-written, synthesiser
"Signs Of Life" June 30, 2017 co-written
"Electric Blue" July 13, 2017 co-written
"Put Your Money On Me" July 28, 2017 co-written, programming

GUY-MANUEL DE HOMEM-CHRISTO

SINGLES

Le Knight Club with Éric Chedeville, AKA Rico The Wizard

"Santa Claus" / "Holiday on Ice" 1997 (Crydamoure)

"Intergalaktic Disko" VS DJ Sneak 1997 (Crydamoure)

"Troobadoor" / "Mirage" 1998 (Crydamoure)

"Boogie Shell"/"Coco Girlz"/"Mosquito"/"Coral Twist" 1999 (Crydamoure)

"Hysteria" 1999 (Crydamoure)

"Think Love, Not Hate" VS DJ Sneak 1999 (Rico The Wizard)

"Gator / Chérie D'Amour" (2001)

"Nymphae Song" / "Rhumba" 2002 (Crydamoure)

"Soul Bells" / "Palm Beat" / "Tropicall" 2002 (Crydamoure)

"The Fight" 2015 (Rico The Wizard)

Crydajam with Éric Chedeville, Paul de Homem-Christo, Cyril Kebellian, Mederic Nebinger, Juan Carlos Pellegrino, J. Vatran, Ouk, Jade, and James Perry.

"If You Give Me The Love I Want"/"Playground"/"Loaded" 2003 (Crydamoure)

COLLABORATION

Raw Man
"*Lovers* "/ "*Number 7*" /"*Number 7*" (Remix by Le Knight Club) 1999 (Crydamoure)

Phoenix
United "Too Young" (Le Knight Club Remix) July 10, 2000 (Source)

Zoot Woman
"Taken It All" *(Le Knight Club Remix)* April 5, 2004 (Wall Of Sound)

Cassius
15 Again "See Me Now" September 11, 2006 (EMI)
drum programming (beat), bass, guitar, synthesiser, producer - Le Knight Club

Sébastien Tellier
Sexuality February 25, 2008 album production
My God Is Blue "My Poseidon" June 5, 2012 (Record Makers) co-written

Kavinsky
OutRun "Nightcall" April 2, 2010 (Record Makers) co-producer

Charlotte Gainsbourg
Rest "Rest" November 17, 2017 (Because Music) produced, music, lyrics co-written

The Weeknd
My Dear Melancholy "Hurt You" March 30, 2018 (XO/Republic) co-written, co-producer

REMIX

David Guetta
Guetta Blaster "Stay" Le Knight Club Remix (Gum Productions/Gum Records) September 16, 2004

Who Is Harris Rosen?

Father. Son. Brother.

Harris Rosen is the author of *N.W.A: The Aftermath, The Real Eminem: Broke City Trash Rapper*, and other Behind The Music Tales books. For twenty years, he self-published the national lifestyle magazine Peace! He lives in Toronto, Canada, with his son, Louis.

Rosen has interviewed hundreds of composers, artists, actors, and athletes. Including the Notorious B.I.G., Dr Dre, Daft Punk, Eminem, Derek Jeter, Georges St. Pierre, Nirvana, Metallica, Chris Rock, Buju Banton, Beastie Boys, Kiss, Destiny's Child and Aaliyah to list a few.

He has gone to six continents and was in the midst of a whirlwind of multiple musical, cultural revolutions that occurred throughout the 90's and 2000s while compiling a genuine and honest archive of audio, images and video.

behindthemusictales.com
Facebook: behindthemusictales
Instagram: behindthemusictales
Twitter: mrheller1

www.ingramcontent.com/pod-product-compliance
Lightning Source LLC
Chambersburg PA
CBHW081500070526
44586CB00019B/2433